THE DEVIL WEARS NADA

THE DEVIL WEARS NADA

Satan Exposed

TRIPP YORK

 CASCADE *Books* · Eugene, Oregon

THE DEVIL WEARS NADA
Satan Exposed

Cascade Books
An Imprint of Wipf and Stock Publishers
199 W. 8th Ave., Suite 3
Eugene, OR 97401

www.wipfandstock.com

ISBN 13: 978-1-60899-560-8

Cataloging-in-Publication data:

York, Tripp.

The devil wears nada : satan exposed / Tripp York.

p. x + 154; cm. Includes bibliographical references.

ISBN 13: 978-1-60899-560-8

1. Devil—Christianity. 2. Devil—Social aspects. 3. United States—History. I. Title

BT982 .467 2011

Manufactured in the U.S.A.

To my father . . .

"You are the kind of boy," the old man said, "that the devil is always going to be offering to assist, to give you a smoke or a drink or a ride, to ask you your business. You had better mind how you take up with strangers. And keep your business to yourself." It was to foil the devil's plans for him that the Lord had seen to his upbringing.

—Flannery O'Connor (*The Violent Bear it Away*)

Contents

ACKNOWLEDGMENTS

Appearances aside, I really am an ecumenist. I can't help it; I'm a team player. Of course, I'm very particular about which team I play for, but I do enjoy having friends on other teams. For me, such ecumenicity extends beyond the realm of Christianity in an effort to find common ground amidst other religious and cultural traditions. This book locates such common ground and then seeks to berate it—all in an effort to expose a larger common ground, that of a certain philosophical persuasion that problematically ties many of us together. In this sense, the Devil is something of a foil employed as the backdrop to my theological musing (and haphazard disabusing) made in order to see what underwrites some of our shared claims about God, the Devil, and everything in-between.

This book would not be possible without the help of a whole lot of friends (along with a few enemies). First, though he should not be held responsible for the content of this book, thank you Tobias Winwright, friend and moral theologian extraordinaire, for the smashingly crafty title. Thanks also to Lynn Barnwell, Amanda Marshall, Tim Weist, Angela Chance, Felicia Dunlap, Brady Plummer, Drew Johnson, Alec Lewis, and Patrick Brandt for their online participation in the search for catchy titles/subtitles. Most of them were terrible, but thanks nonetheless.

Many thanks to Joshua London, who is a testimony to the intelligibility of paganism (and yes, that's a compliment). To Bruce Schulte, who is a testimony to the intelligibility of biology (and yes, that too is a compliment). Thanks to Chip Barnette and Joe Baker, whose knowledge of music knows no limitations, and because of which the world is a better place (long live "The Fabulous Paramounts"—thanks David Wright). Thank you Tracy Jo Ingram and Meredith Wadlington for laboriously pouring over this manuscript and making it readable. Many thanks to my good friend Matt Litton who is as excited about this book as I am (that's only because he has yet to read it), and to Andrew Bergman whose commentary on the "V" on the cover will always haunt me. I also owe a debt of gratitude to Chuck Seay and Scott Thomas. The kinds of conversations I have had through the years with you two are irreplaceable. Your contributions to this book cannot be overstated.

The completion of this book occurred during my second year of teaching at Western Kentucky University. The folks in the Philosophy and Religion Department have been especially kind as I transitioned from the fine state of North Carolina to the almost equally fine state of Kentucky. To Eric Bain-Selbo, for graciously extending to me your classrooms; Jeffery Samuels, for your recommendations in Thai food; Arvin Vos, for teaching Aquinas; Ingrid Lilly, for just being Ingrid Lilly; Paula Williams, for, literally, knowing everything; and to Scott Girdner, a simple request: please stop having kids so we can skate again.

To Charlie Collier, Halden Doerge, Christian Amondson, and the wonderful staff at Wipf & Stock, thanks for taking on another one of my books. You would think they would know better by now. I am greatly indebted to the generosity of the Sinderbrands: Paul, Marilyn, and Carly (Tatiana) are ridiculously good to me. As always, my appreciation to my parents for their patience with their youngest child cannot be overstated. Thanks are also in order to my brother, Danny, who did not give up on AC/DC (despite the warnings from televangelists), and to my sister, Cherie, for always being such a good conversation partner. Finally, to all of the ministers, pastors, priests, clerics, Satanists, pagans, wiccans, bodybuilders, and so many others: thank you for tolerating my persistent badgering. I'm sure I was as bad as some of these interviews make me out to be, and, for that, I apologize. For those of you who yelled at me, raised a fist, refused to call me back, sent vicious emails, or even placed hexes on me, you know who you are . . . and so does Satan.

Tripp York
Bowling Green, Kentucky

The devil divides the world between atheism and superstition.
—George Herbert

INTRODUCTION

That's nonsense. I invented electricity. Ben Franklin is the Devil!
—Mama Boucher

"Be careful what you wish for," cautioned Brother Ray, "you just might get it." Brother Ray, whose name (along with a few others in this book) has been changed to protect him from possible evil repercussions, was dutifully concerned with the scope of my project. "Why on earth," he asked, "would anyone in their right mind want to find *him*?"

I immediately recorded the first observation in my research: Satan, it seems, has testicles.

Before I could respond, he added, with a touch of baffled sincerity, "Good Lord boy, what's wrong with you?"

I looked at this man who had lived a hard life of some sixty-plus years (and whose sideburns suggested a slight obsession with the King of Rock & Roll) and replied, "What's wrong with me? Brother Ray, like so many other people on this rotating rock, I just want to find God."

An occasion for nuance may be in order. I'm not claiming that some ontological personality referred to as Satan is God or is even a god. Despite the deification of Satan by religious people of various stripes, this was not my point. I have simply decided that my research should take a more indirect approach. So much of what passes for a person's search for God tends to be located in one of two frameworks: personal experience or apologetic precision.

In regards to the former, it is important to note that many people across a variety of cultures, times, and places have stressed one-on-one experiences with something referred to as the divine. Of course, countless scholars have constructed countless theories for such a phenomenon. Regardless of their validity, or lack thereof, I have no interest in repeating such theories here. At this point it may simply be enough to point out that the biggest problem with this form of knowledge is the limitations of anything self-referential. Everyone's personal experience is just that— his or her personal experience. How such an experience is helpful for me is never quite clear, as what makes something subjective is, well, its subjectivity.

We also run into a serious quandary if one's faith in God is predicated on his or her personal experience. Such predication lacks any means of negotiating the differences between a Hindu's experience with Shiva (or any of the other 329,999 gods), a Jew's experience with YHWH, a Muslim's experience with Allah, a Christian's experience with Jesus, or an animist's experience with river nymphs. Since I'm not an imperialist, I refuse to chalk all of these experiences up to the same thing. Though Western pluralists fancy themselves tolerant and inclusive in their suggestion that all religions are manifestations of the same reality, I can think of nothing more exclusivistic than the claim that Muslims, Christians, and Shintoists, for example, adore the same reality. Try telling that to any devout practitioners of these traditions and they will certainly not find such a claim to be tolerant, but exceedingly pretentious. After all, what lofty philosophical mountaintops would one need to occupy to make such a judgment? How would anyone possibly verify the truth of such a claim?

Getting back to one's own subjective knowledge, let it be known that I know people whose personal experience reading a well-written comic book was enough for them to warrant belief in God. Granted, the works of Gaiman, Moore, Eisner, and Vaughn are quite good, but perhaps not *that* good. Speaking for myself, I have probably never been surer of the existence of God than when West Virginia University beat the University of Kentucky only to be thoroughly pummeled by the eventual champions of the NCAA Basketball Championship of 2010, the Duke University Blue Devils. This reconfirmed my suspicions about the existence of God from a previous experience when I was on Duke University's campus in April of 2001. Again, for greatness is repetitive, we had just won the NCAA Basketball Championship, which not only proved the existence of God, but also God's denominational affiliation—Methodist.

Indeed, the major flaw I see in people's personal experiences (mine included) as *the* decider or arbiter in belief in a benevolent deity is that feeling good (or blessed) lends itself to Feuerbachian criticism. The eighteenth-century philosopher Ludwig Feuerbach argued that humans were not created in the image of God; rather, we created God in our image.[1] Humans, Feuerbach argued, merely project their desires, needs, and wishes onto an imaginary deity that proceeds to fulfill such desires, needs, and wishes. One does not need to be an atheist to see the potential truth in such an argument. Historically, Christianity has rightly criticized the same thing and, to a point, agrees with Feuerbach. Many people's understanding of God often coincides with the kind of deity they most desire. In this rubric, God, coincidentally, just happens to bless the kind of life we already wanted to live. God makes us feel good, and it makes us feel good that the God of all creation wants us to want what we already wanted. What a wonderful deity to be so concerned with our feeling good about our self-appointed lives! Of course, to paraphrase the religious psychologist William James, if merely "feeling good" could decide the authenticity of our truth claims, then drunkenness would be the supremely valid human experience. You will therefore have to forgive me for my reluctance to base my knowledge of God on your personal experiences.

In the case of the more apologetic believer in our midst—where knowledge of God comes, perhaps, from philosophical precision—I find even less hope. To speak crudely, the god of the philosophers is rarely the god of any of the so-called world religions. The god whose existence is proven and disproven by academicians is rarely the god anyone actually believes in. The god criticized in the cosmological argument or the god who "intelligently designed" the cosmos has little to nothing in common with, for example, the God of Jesus worshipped by Christians. What passes for proof and disproof seems to just miss the point altogether.

Take, for example, the argument from design: Even if you concede that the universe is far too complex to have evolved via adaptation and natural selection, and, therefore, you find it necessary to posit the exis-

1. See Ludwig Feuerbach, trans. Alexander Loos, *The Essence of Christianity* (Amherst: Prometheus, 2004).

tence of a creator, such a proof tells you nothing *about* the creator. What am I to worship—the Intelligent Designer? Well, what does that look like? Such a proof tells me nothing about the character of the deity proven to exist. It is the same thing with the cosmological argument. The cosmological argument claims that all things are contingent upon something else for its existence, yet if we assume a beginning in time then there must be one non-contingent being, and that one non-contingent being is God. Even if this were to convince an unbeliever that God exists (and arguments for the existence of God have the uncanny tendency to convince only those who need no convincing), this does not tell me anything about the non-contingent being proven to exist.

The Greek philosopher Aristotle referred to this non-contingent being as the Unmoved Mover. Well, that's just great. How am I supposed to worship the Unmoved Mover? What shape or form would such worship take? Does the Unmoved Mover punish people for certain actions or reward others for other actions? Does the Unmoved Mover grow angry when I massacre my time, and brain cells, watching *Days of Our Lives*? Or, is the Unmoved Mover genuinely concerned with "Bo" and "Hope" finding true happiness? How would I possibly ever know?

The problem with such arguments is that if they do convince you of God's existence they only convince you of what you already were going to be, or needed to be convinced of in the first place. Taken on their own terms, they tell you nothing about the kind of deity "proven" to exist. For that reason alone, I just cannot muster any interest in such arguments.

So, what am I attempting to do by saying I am looking for God by looking for Satan? Are the subjective experiences and the philosophical arguments for God so bad and uninteresting that I would be willing to confront the Prince of Lies (therein making my search paradoxically problematic) in order to learn of God's existence?

Yes. I honestly think they are that bad and uninteresting.

I have spent quite a few years teaching at a private liberal arts university, as well as at a much larger public university, and have grown quite weary of how utterly predictable every argument, claim, and comment my students make about God turn out to be (no offense to past or present students—it's not your fault). The god so often discussed and assumed by many of my students, taught to them by their parents, rabbis, imams, priests, preachers, politicians, and marketing consultants, is a god of banal platitudes who apparently exists for no other reason than to make them feel good about decisions they were already going to make. This god is a god who wants all of us to be wealthy and healthy and to find the perfect soul mate.

Pretty swell deity—albeit a thoroughly pagan one.

Of course, this should not be taken as criticism against the possible existence of God. It is not that at all. Rather, it's because I truly hope that, if the God of Judaism, Islam, and/or Christianity is real, then such a God would have to be far more compelling than the trite and mawkish god I am informed—through the channels of whimsical personal experience and logical reasoning of others—exists. So you see, I am not challenging the existence of God, I am challenging the god thought to exist.

THE WAGER:
WHY TOMMY NO LONGER WORKS ON THE DOCKS

Perhaps that last comment belongs in a book that I will one day write. This is not that book. At least, I don't think this is that book. What I wish to do is attempt to capitalize on a particular conversation held in one of my Introduction to Religious Studies courses that inspired me to search for Satan as a way of knowing God.

My class was working through some of the arguments I was previously alluding to (argument by design, cosmological argument, etc.), and we were criticizing not only the arguments for the existence of God, but also the arguments against the arguments for the existence of God. The class was moving in a manner that seemed almost pre-programmed.[2] Then, a strange thing happened; something new began to develop between two of my more fervent students. They were discussing whether or not one could really know, and I mean *know* in the sense that I know I am typing these words on paper, that God exists. It was, at first, a polite conversation, but it suddenly took a turn for the unexpected. The believer refused to relent on the notion that one can know that God exists despite not being able to articulate how others can know *as* she knows. It was at this point that things became a little more interesting. I will attempt to

2. It's inevitable. No matter how many times I cover this material, my so-called free-thinking and hyper-individualistic students unfailingly rehash the same old stale arguments.

paraphrase the conversation as best as my memory will allow. For the sake of anonymity, I will refer to the two students as Tommy and Gina (with heartfelt apologies to Bon Jovi):

Tommy: Do you believe in Satan?

Gina: Of course.

Tommy: Do you think you can prove the existence of Satan?

Gina: Well, I'm not sure why that would be necessary . . .

Tommy: I'm just wondering: if your proof of God's existence is based on your experience with God then is it also necessary for you to experience Satan in order for you to know that Satan exists?

Gina: If you are suggesting that I have been possessed then I don't appreciate such a . . . what did you call it Dr. York?

Professor (*that's me.*): I think you are intimating that Tommy is attempting to engage in an *ad hominem* argument. That is an attack against the person as opposed to their argument. We agreed, at the beginning of class, that out of respect for one another we would avoid such attacks.

Gina: Right.

Tommy: No, that's not what I'm doing. I was just asking how you can know that a supernatural being like Satan exists if in order to know that God exists you must have a personal experience with God.

Gina: Well, I know Satan exists because I know God exists.

Professor: A sort of knowledge via association?

Gina: Sure. If I believe that God exists then I have to believe the things God says, and Scripture makes it clear that Satan exists. It seems pretty obvious.

Tommy: It does to me, too. So, since we are incapable of proving, at least to my satisfaction, that God exists, do you think it's possible to prove that Satan exists, therein requiring me, via association, as the good doctor put it, to believe in God? I mean, Christians are always warning one another to be on the lookout for the Devil, so if I had an experience with Satan, or if I were possessed by Satan, then I would have to believe in God, right?

Gina: You may be possessed for even thinking that way.

Professor: Now Gina, as quick and witty as that comment was, and everyone here knows how much I appreciate "quick and witty," that was an engagement with the very tactic you were accusing Tommy of employing.

Tommy: Thanks Doc. Look, all I'm saying is that you Christians are seriously worried about Satan tempting you to do bad things, and possessing you, and all that, right?

Gina: Right.

Tommy: So, it must not be that difficult to come under Satan's influence, right?

Gina: No . . . I don't think so.

Tommy: Do you think Satan would come into my heart if I asked him to?

Gina (*who hesitantly answers such an oft-putting question*): Yes. But why would—

Tommy: Because then I would know! Isn't that genius? Then I would know that God exists, because I know that Satan exists! It would so be worth it. Totally worth it. So, what do I have to do to have an experience with Satan?

Gina: I think you're having one.

Professor: Gina.

Gina: Sorry. (*This next comment is directed toward me.*) It's just that, the more I think about it, the more I believe I am quite fond of *ad hominem* arguments.

Professor: Actually, me too. I have always insisted that you should not be able to separate the argument from the person attempting to embody the argument, but for the sake of common courtesy, you are not allowed to use them. They must be saved for political campaigns and graduate school.

Gina: Fair enough. (*Turning back to Tommy.*) I don't know. I've never tried to summon the Devil, but it seems that all you have to do is want him to rule your life and he will do it.

Tommy: So, what do I do, I mean, specifically?

Gina: I said "I don't know." How would I know? I guess just ask him to possess you and he won't be able resist.

Tommy: Then I'll do it. Fifty times a day for as long as it takes. Doc, can you schedule an exorcism if necessary?

Professor: Hold on a second. Let it be clear that I am neither approving nor condoning this experiment—.

Tommy: Oh, come on. I have the opportunity to know that God exists, and if God is who everyone says he is then he can rid the Devil from me and then I'm golden. I'm doing it. And then, when it doesn't happen, when this demonic being that your tradition feels like it has to constantly pray to God in order to resist does not possess someone wanting to be possessed, then I will know that this is all nonsense. (*Extending his hand to Gina.*) Come on, shake on it. I'll risk possession in order to know that what you claim to know is knowable. (*He thinks about that for a second.*) What did I just say? Was that right?

Professor: Sounded good. It was very poetic. Nicely done.

Tommy: Thanks. And if I don't end up being possessed, you have to admit that I'm right, and no one can know whether or not God exists, and that actually this may be an argument against the existence of God. Deal?

Gina: No . . . no, wait, that's crazy, because Satan knows why you're doing it, and since Satan doesn't want you to believe in God then he won't make himself known to you.

Tommy: Let me get this straight: you can be possessed by Satan because you believe in God, but because I don't believe in God I can't be possessed by Satan? Sounds like you're the one getting the raw end of the deal. (*Touché Tommy, touché.*)

Gina: No, you can be possessed . . . you can, all right? You just won't be. I'm just saying that because of your reasons for it, Satan will not do anything to prove his existence.

Tommy: Oh, this is so typical. First you claim you have to beg to keep Satan away, but yet if I go looking for him he disappears. Maybe *I* should be an exorcist.

At this point the conversation fell into a stalemate. We reached an impasse by which neither student was capable of convincing the other of the superiority of their reasoning skills. If I had been keeping score I would have awarded Tommy the victory. Gina, I imagine, would protest, claiming that Tommy may have won this battle, but he would surely lose the war.

After a day or two I forgot about their argument. A few weeks went by and, for some reason, I suddenly remembered Tommy's proposal. I asked him, outside of class, if he went through with it. He told me that he gave it a shot on the first night, but was called away on more pressing matters.

I think it had something to do with an Xbox 360.

Like most college students, his interest in thought experiments outside the classroom quickly dissipated. Perhaps that's a good thing.

Maybe it was divine intervention.

Yet, the more I think about it, the more I am convinced it is not a half-bad idea (which means, admittedly, it is only a half-good idea). Not that I want to be possessed by the Devil, assuming such an entity exists, it is just the idea that with so much emphasis some religious traditions place on this creature's ability to wreak havoc in the world, then perhaps there is something to Tommy's wager. Perhaps traditional pursuits of God are not the most efficient. What if we went on a search for Satan in order to shed light on the existence, and, possibly, the character of God?

"So Brother Ray, that's all I'm doing. That's why I need you to help me come to terms with this Satan character."

Appearing rather offended, he asked, "Well, why in the world would you think I would be of any help in that department?"

"I'm glad you asked," I told him. "I was thinking that since your sermon, stellar by the way, mentioned Satan as many times as it mentioned Jesus—Jesus received seventy-eight honorable mentions, Satan ninety-six . . . give or take a few—I thought you could help me make a connection. What do you say?"

"Son," stated a flabbergasted lamb-chopped Brother Ray, "I'm afraid you might already be under his influence."

For some reason, I thought of Gina.

1 THE PROTESTANT DEIFICATION OF THE DEVIL

I have always felt friendly toward Satan. Of course, that is ancestral; it must be in the blood, for I could not have originated it.

—Mark Twain

Hell is empty, and all the devils are down here.

—Ariel (William Shakespeare, *The Tempest*)

Throughout the course of my research, the one thing I have discovered is that Protestants love talking about Satan. They simply cannot get enough of him.

To be sure, there are those highbrow liturgical Protestants who think themselves far too respectable to be caught dead attributing certain travesties to the Prince of Darkness; but, as you can imagine, those folks are of little use to me. Nevertheless, I'll return to a few of them later.

For now, however, I am interested in the majority of Protestants that fueled my upbringing and continue to geographically surround me. The Protestant South has an undoubted love affair with the diabolical one. That pointy-eared chief of demons seems to be responsible for every single tragedy, calamity, and mishap in the world. If you doubt the authenticity of such a claim, I have included an abbreviated list of things that Satan has supposedly been responsible for—and I am restricting this to *only* a small number of comments I have had the good fortune of hearing. The Devil has:

- unplugged a screen projector
- encouraged people to vote for Bill Clinton

- created albinos (the red eyes, I guess)
- introduced thoughts of impurity to everyone but my Sunday School teacher
- made watermelons taste like tomatoes (they really did)
- led Michael English to have an adulterous affair
- possessed the Pope, Jane Fonda, and Gorbachev
- inspired the creation of South Park, Will & Grace, and Three's Company (RIP John Ritter, I hope you're not in hell)
- can change the color of things
- is "behind" homosexuality (see chapter 2)
- gave the Yankees victory over the South (for possession of their Northern souls of course)
- married some of my relatives (I actually believe that one)
- occasionally wears a blue dress
- caused microphone feedback
- crossed the street disguised as a black cat
- carried a dead man away at a wake (while my intoxicated grandfather and his blitzed cousins just sat there and watched)
- gave one of my friends a lisp
- created the Smurfs
- took Jesse Helms from this earth "way too early" (or wait, was that God?)
- caused spelling errors in church bulletins
- created Islam
- created the internet (sorry Al Gore, unless . . .)
- is aiding the Chinese "take over" of America
- created puppets (okay, that one is mine—I hate puppets)
- invented Halloween
- tempts Catholics to worship Mary and other saints
- tempts women to work outside the home
- promotes dancing which leads to sex ("What kind of dancing?" I asked. "Salsa? Swing? The Jitterbug?" The Nazarene minister replied, "*All* dancing leads to sex." Which, of course, immediately convinced me to engage in all forms of dancing. Let it be known, that minister lied to me.)
- and for the grand finale (sans the purported aphrodisiac of dancing, no less), forced me to have sex prior to marriage . . . sorry mom, Satan made me do it.

This short list alone is a testament to what appears to be Satan's almost infinite power. If his abilities to pull off the above, often times simultaneously, does not make him a god, then I'm not sure what would.

"He's still answerable to the God that created him, young man!" This is a fairly predictable theological truism. Every time I tried to make the point that Satan's power seems to be encroaching on God's power, I would hear something to the effect of, "The only power he has is the power God allows him to have."

That's an interesting claim.

So, whom do I really blame for the unplugged projector and funky tasting watermelons? Satan or God?

"That's borderline blasphemy," protested an Assembly of God minister.

"No," I said, "that's a problem of providence."

THE DEVIL IS MY DJ:
THE REAL FRESH PRINCE OF BAAL AIR

In Jesus' name, we pray for no microphone problems!
—Becky Fischer (*Jesus Camp*)

The following act attributed to Satan occurred in a Nazarene church. A bit of biography is in order: I was raised by the Nazarenes. I joined the Mennonite Church about a decade ago, and they have been paying the price ever since. Mennonites, at least the ones I've been around (think urban weirdoes as opposed to rural weirdoes), speak very little about Satan. We have found that humans are more than capable of perpetrating acts of evil without the help of a lesser deity. The Nazarenes, however, are ultimately responsible for my obsession with all things theological. They are the ones responsible for putting the fear of God (and Satan) in me.

They also put in me the fear of sex, wine, tobacco, cards, gambling, dancing, movie theaters, mixed bathing (that's co-ed swimming for the uninitiated), and any music not written by the Gaithers.

The last of these being the easiest to overcome.

As a child I was terrified of the incessant stories of the Devil and demonic possession. The pastor of my youthful years—a wonderful man, very humble and ripe with conviction—instructed us that the Devil was a roaring lion waiting to infiltrate our lives at any given moment. Despite being tempted by the Devil to not pay attention to his sermons, many of them, for good and/or bad, still haunt me. Problems, however, started to arise whenever I had to go to bed. I recall that on many nights during my childhood, I literally begged God to keep Satan from abducting or possessing me while I tried to sleep.

Ironic, right? Now I'm searching for him.

So there I was, having come full-circle; no longer a Nazarene, yet sitting in a Nazarene church wondering if *he* was going to show up. Was this church truly big enough for Jesus and the Devil? However, as I gazed across the layout of the church, I began to wonder to myself, would either one even *want* to show up?

Aesthetically, it was a flat-out disaster. Many Protestant churches have so completely devoured the church-growth strategies in vogue over the past several decades that it is no longer intelligible even to have a conversation about the aesthetics of sacred spaces. Part of this movement is making churches look less like churches and more like a combination of warehouses and office buildings. Pews are out, comfortable chairs are in (so Protestant—always glorifying the individual). Hymnals have been burned (or donated[1]) and, in their place, meaningless lyrics shallow enough to embarrass contestants on The Bachelor are projected on a huge white screen. Crosses are often hidden, as they are such a downer, but the coffee bars seem to have assuaged most would-be complainers. Everything is very sanitary. Clean walls, clean carpet, and the smell of newness permeate the contemporary church, meticulously designed to attract an insatiable and fickle consumer.

These people really need to read the works of Chuck Palahniuk.

As the church leaders began orchestrating a show bent on leading me into a depoliticized and privatized experience with my very own per-

---

1. To whom? What actually happens with all those unwanted hymnals? Perhaps the "younger evangelicals" are repurposing these castaway collections in their efforts to get in touch with some semblance of tradition. It's odd to imagine, but it could just be that yesterday's kids are finding use for the hymns their parents no longer find meaningful. Wouldn't have seen that one coming as a teenager when I was forced to sing the tenor parts to classics like, "It Is Well with My Soul."

sonal Jesus (and no, I don't like Depeche Mode), I thought about how silly the protest is against high liturgical church services. Many, even mainstream, churches claim that high liturgical services are too rigid and far too ordered. It is commonly suggested that they do not remain open to the movement of the Holy Spirit. Yet, in all of my countless experiences with the burgeoning church growth movement, which currently dominates groups like the Pentecostals, Nazarenes, Methodists, the so-called non-Denominational churches (which is code for general moralism while furthering the ignorance of one's own tradition), and every other church compelled to entertain their patrons, I feel as if they owe a sincere apology to Catholics and Episcopalians. Seriously, your typical Pentecostal or contemporary worship service is just as rigorously structured as the Catholic Mass. Now I'm aware that many people would disagree with this claim. For example, the youth/music pastor at a Presbyterian ARP Church told me their music was never "pre-programmed" and was always a last-second decision. When I asked him about his choice of Sunday morning music he explained to me that he didn't even pick the songs.

"If you don't choose the songs, then who does?" I asked.

"Dude, let me tell you something," he said to me. "That's not me up there singing and playing those songs. That's Jesus. Give him the glory."

Okay, ignoring the obvious problems with this, let it be said that I am more than willing to give Jesus serious props for lots of things, including:

- healing the blind, lame, and deaf
- bringing the dead back to life
- his ability to walk on water
- turning over tables and chasing people with whips for capitalizing on one's religion (I think its past time for a repeat performance)
- hanging out with prostitutes
- his ability to phase through walls
- turning water into wine (praise Jesus)
- and enduring that whole crucifix ordeal which Mel Gibson opportunistically seized in order to share with millions his predilection for anti-Semitism and sadistic violence.

But I just can't attribute the *having of an idea* to sing the average fetishized and maudlin love song with lyrics like "I just want you to touch me deep down inside" to Jesus. Sorry, not going to happen.

Back to the Nazarenes.

The lights remained bright on the stage/pulpit as the lights dimmed over the audience/parishioners, giving me the feeling that this whole experience could be on par with your average community-theater performance. Even worse, I had that feeling one gets when they hear their local high school drama department is going to do *Guys and Dolls*—again.

Uncomfortably, I watched as women in face paint and spiritually accessorized men contorted their bodies, shed crocodile tears, and gave one another and Jesus high fives while the guitarist, who clearly was impressed with himself, nailed that three-chord progression so prevalent in Christian worship-pop.[2] I kept thinking that if the Greeks got it right—that is, if truth, goodness, and beauty are intertwined in such a way that you cannot have one without the other—and if Jesus is the Truth, then why would he possibly bother hanging around such a superficially constructed and theologically barren atmosphere? Whatever it is that Jesus stands for, it cannot be this banal, right? I mean, he was an executed criminal. People wanted him dead because of his views on money. Please tell me he died for something more interesting than producing a church movement that does little more than increase the wealth of a few dozen people in "Contemporary Christian Nashville."

Tangent aside, I am still here and waiting to see if one of the two will show. And while I couldn't verify the whereabouts of Jesus, I was pleased to see that Satan made an appearance. At about the midway point of the "praise service," the CD with the accompanying musical tracks for the soloist started to skip. As the CD was skipping, the pastor quickly informed the congregation, in what I understood to be an attempt to bide a little time so the sound technicians could get things under control, that the "Devil is working extra hard today to keep us from praising Jesus' name. But it's not going to work Devil. You should just know that right now. It's not going to work, Devil."

He stated the next three sentences very slowly, deliberately, and with an increasing sense of urgency, "It is not going to work. You should just leave right now. You can't stop us from praising his holy name!"

And the crowd went wild.

As the pastor was relaying his message to the Prince of Darkness, the majority of the congregation was in an uproar of agreement. "Amens"

---

2. Thank you, Michael W. Smith.

and "Praise the Lords" were tossed around with a more fervent spirit than when the CD was actually playing.

I can't lie to you; I was actually excited.

To find out that Satan was in the building, at that very moment, felt like an opportunity worth seizing. Unfortunately, by the time I could figure out how to make the most of my opportunity, the sound engineer in the back of the church shouted, "We're good to go. Take it away!"

The pastor, a white, middle-aged man who appeared to be relatively uninformed about the Christian practice of fasting, informed us that the Devil had been defeated (those sound guys were good!) and was nowhere to be found.

"Oh, well," I thought. I guess I missed him. But, apparently some other folks, who must have been far more spiritually in tune with the forces of evil than I am, felt his presence. After the service, I decided I would ask the pastor about it.

Fast forward through a sermon on the virtues of *The Andy Griffith Show*, as well as eight teary-eyed choruses, and church was finally over. I asked the pastor if I could have a few moments of his time outside the obligatory handshake offered on the way out. He consented, and we made our way to his office.

I began the discussion by asking the pastor if he could talk to me a little bit about Satan, his demonic strategies, and how to avoid them. I thanked him for meeting with me, and I told him I understood such a subject to be a bit peculiar.

"Not at all," he told me. "However I can help increase another person in the knowledge of the Lord, I am happy to do so."

"'Increase another person' . . . what?"

"What's that?" he asked.

"Nothing, nothing. I'm just interested in what appears to be, though I must be getting this wrong, the seemingly omnipresent status of the Devil."

"Well," the pastor stated, "he is the ruler of the air."

"Ephesians chapter 2, correct?"

"That sounds about right to me," he confided.

"I guess my more immediate question is this: Why is it the case that some Christians are more aware of Satan, or the Devil—I'm going to use those two terms interchangeably if that is okay with you—why is—

"It's the same person," he interrupted, "so why wouldn't you?"

"Right, sure. Of course, there are some historical differences and a clear development that occurs between the Old Testament and the New Testament, but . . . wait, are you saying that Satan is a person?"

"Well, no, of course not," he responded. "Satan is a fallen angel. I just said that because there is no need to obsess with the carefulness of our words."

"Yeah. The curse of doing graduate work is that in order to obtain the degree we have to obsess with speaking carefully."

He laughed as if that were a joke.

"That can eat up a lot of valuable time," he told me. "Time that should be properly used giving glory to God. You agree?"

Wait a second. Did he just take a shot at my education? I think he did. Awesome. Admittedly, my education is not without fault. For one thing, it was terribly overpriced. So his shot was not without merit. But hey, at least at this point I knew our conversation was going to be interesting.

I attempted to defend myself by suggesting that anyone willing to spend most of their life in higher education, learning as much about Christianity, her doctrines, her history, and the God she worships, would, as crazy as it must sound, be time well spent.

"Such service," I explained, "is itself a form of prayer. Actually, it was a Nazarene professor who instilled that notion in me. Plus, Augustine and Aquinas argued along those very lines, and that's coming from two of the most influential theologians our church has ever produced. Do you not agree?"

He quickly attempted to assure me he was not trying to demean my studies, but was only pointing out that "education doesn't always translate into the kind of love Jesus requires of his disciples."

"Well," I conceded, "there is no disagreement on that point."

"Right."

"Right. Okay, so, my question is this: Why is it the case that some Christians are aware of the presence of Satan in a way that others are not? I mean, is that a gift? To feel the presence of Satan?"

With a hearty and incredibly patronizing laugh he responded, "Talking about speaking carefully, I'm not sure I would call that a gift. Though there's all kinds of gifts in the church, and I guess you could say that some people, more so than others, are more properly in tune with what the forces of evil are up to."

"You mean like messing with CD players?"

"What's that?" he asked, as he had to think about it for a second. Suddenly remembering he said, "Oh, yes. Well, sure. Sure. Why not? He's trying to interrupt our worship service. Satan hates it when people praise the name of Jesus. He does everything in his power to stop it. Anything is fair game for the Devil."

"Then why does he even show up?" I asked. "I mean, if he hates it so much, and he is powerful enough to apparently be in a whole lot of places, perhaps all places, at once, not to mention his uncanny ability to poke a stick in the wheel of technology, then it seems he would be capable of just not listening."

"Well, that's part of his punishment. He is forced to listen to God's people singing the Lord's praises."

"Well," I admitted, "I can definitely see how that would be a cruel form of punishment."

He nodded. Unwittingly, I assumed.

"Could you point me to a text?" I asked.

"What's that?"

"A text? Well, a text is another word for a book or a section of a book. I—"

"I know what a text is," he interrupted. "I'm asking you what you mean by pointing to a text."

"Oh, well, you said that part of Satan's punishment is he is forced to listen to Christians sing God's praises, so I was wondering if you could point me to a piece of Scripture, some authoritative text, that says, 'And I will punish you by forcing you to listen to Christians sing choruses?'"

Defensively he said, "I think it is fairly common knowledge that Satan hates any kind of praising or worshipping of God. He can't be in the presence of it."

"So, what you are saying is that when your church starts praising God, Satan has no choice but to flee?"

"That's right," he answered.

"Well, and I hope you will pardon my inability to catch on, but if that's the case, what was he still doing there halfway through the service?"

"Come again?"

"The CD," I reminded him, "didn't start skipping until halfway through the service, so I'm wondering why Satan was still there."

"Well, now son," he said with more than a touch of condescension, "I think you're taking this all a bit too literally."

Sensing the blossoming enmity occurring in our conversation, I responded, "I admit to not knowing the difference between taking something literally and taking something 'too literally,' I'm not entirely sure what that means, but that's beside the point. Are you telling me you don't believe in the existence of Satan?"

"Of course, I do," he said. "You can't be a Christian and not believe in Satan."

That is a very fascinating theological claim. I was always under the impression it had more to do with Jesus, but before I could ask him about it he said, "That's the first trick of Satan, you know?"

Oh, how I know. This will be the gazillionth time I've been told, "The first trick of the Devil is to convince you he doesn't exist." I can already tell that this is going to be an ongoing struggle I will have to face throughout my research.

"Yeah, that's what I keep hearing," I responded. "But back to what you said about me taking things literally. I'm a little confused because you said that part of Satan's punishment is to be forced to listen to Christians sing, yet when Satan hears God being praised he has to flee, so I'm not sure how to reconcile that conundrum . . . and then the whole thing with the CD."

"Right, so yes," he replied in what was quickly becoming a frustrated tone. "Satan is being punished yet attempts to escape his punishment through either distracting us from our worship services or, if that fails, fleeing, but, you know, at the same time, everything that happens, or every little thing that goes wrong, doesn't necessarily mean Satan is responsible."

"Oh. That's strange, because when the CD started skipping you attributed it to Satan. Was that a moment utilized in the service of metaphor or were you speaking literally? Because it seemed like the congregation understood it quite literally."

"Well, yes," he confessed, "it was Satan trying to disrupt our service."

"You really attribute a scratch on a CD to Satan?"[3]

"Of course not," he said. "But Satan definitely attempts to thwart our plans to serve God. That's what Satan does."

"I'm confused. Please forgive me for pushing this issue, but did Satan scratch the CD or not?"

---

3. Note to self: hide CD collection.

"No, now look," he said, growing exhausted by this line of questioning. "We don't even know if it was a scratch. Who said it was scratched? There could of have been any number of reasons why the CD was skipping."

"But any number of those reasons," I kept pushing, "could be, ultimately, traced back to Satan?"

"Yes. Exactly."

He was looking at his watch as if to let me know our time together was coming to a close. I knew I was losing him, and despite wanting him to clarify his rather conflicting responses, I elected to go all in while he was still with me.

"Do you think I could meet him?"

At this point, he was overtaken with annoyance. He asked if this whole conversation was a joke and if this was just a game academicians play with those who do the "real work" of making disciples.

I tried to convince him it was not my intention to play games. I told him I was only trying to make sense out of what I experienced in his service. "As a pastor," I said, "you should be anxious to answer these questions. Paul tells us to be prepared to answer—"

"I know what Paul says," he interrupted, "but I seriously doubt he had in mind Christians wanting to have a meeting with Satan. I'm pretty sure he would think that indicative of a much larger problem."

"Yeah, that's probably true," I conceded.

I actually appreciated being called out on that point. That was him being a good pastor.

"But, when I asked you about meeting Satan I didn't necessarily assume you exercised such power or control, it was more of a rhetorical way of . . . well, I guess you can say that I'm just very fascinated with your ability to know and feel the presence of Satan in your church, because I couldn't. I would not have had any idea that Satan was here today had you not informed us. Therefore, I assume you have some kind of connection that I presently lack and I was just wondering how I could make such a connection. I mean, apparently that's not a bad thing, because if it were a bad thing then you yourself would not have the connection. But you do, and I feel like I don't. So, I'm asking for an 'in.'"

The only "in" I received was the "end" of our conversation.

He abruptly cut me off and told me he was late for lunch or a committee meeting or something. He also said something about his knowing better than to attempt to have a conversation with someone like me whose only purpose was to tear down and not edify, which, by the way, I find patently false. I am all about edification. I'm just opposed to the kind of edification that one cannot, under a simple line of questioning, articulate and defend. It makes us look bad. The least we should be able to do is tolerate a few questions of clarification. All I was asking is that if he can feel the presence of the Devil in his services could he tell me how, so that I could better relay this information to others in order to lead more people to God? I know, I know. I'm sure that sounds messed up—attempting to encounter Satan in order to grow closer to God.

I bet they don't teach that in seminary.

Unfortunately, the more I delve into this project the more I realize that a prerequisite to knowing Satan may be knowing God. Maybe Tommy was right. Maybe Satan only comes with the whole belief-in-God package. In that respect, perhaps we are safer not knowing God. At least then we cannot come under Satan's influence. But if that's true, it only reconfirms the intelligibility of this experiment, because it means that in knowing Satan, I also open myself up to the possibility of knowing God, right?

Right?

Maybe.

DECAPITATED CHICKENS . . . IT'S A METAPHOR

It was the Christians who gave the Devil almost the presence of a god.

—Richard Cavendish

One of my professors at Trevecca Nazarene University once stated, "Evangelicals seem to always be in desperate need of an enemy." I take this to refer to their penchant for being defined more by what they are against than what they are for. This very well may be the case, though I would by no means limit this practice to evangelicals. Whether it is liberals or conservatives, Christians or pagans, anarchists or theocrats, Duke fans and everyone else, the tendency to be defined more by what you are against than what you are for is always tantalizing. In terms of Satan, I think it very well may be the tendency of many Christians to fall prey to this sort of trap. This was not only obvious during much of my upbringing, and I believe in some regards to the previous conversation, but also in my university setting. Granted, many students who attended Trevecca while I was there came from very pious Nazarene backgrounds, so it was hardly surprising to find students who had never been to a movie, a concert (except for the horror of "Carman"), went dancing, or smoked a cigarette. These latter two activities I can only assume were created by the Devil since engaging in them landed you either a fine or placed on social probation.

This tendency to be defined by what you are against was regularly reinforced by the school's choice of speakers in their mandatory chapel services. For instance, during my first year at Trevecca we had a revivalist come to our school for a week. For many students, revivals provided the opportunity to rekindle that fire with God so vital to Christian discipleship. For some of us religion majors, revivals were an opportunity for us to dissect and analyze the content of the preacher. This was, in a sense, part of our training, and I was happy to put my newly apprenticed skills to work. I was excited about attending this revival. I wasn't excited because I thought I was going to experience that Nazarene holy grail known as entire sanctification; I had other reasons. You see, there was a bit of controversy before it even began. Prior to the arrival of the evangelist, a number of his intercessory crew showed up at our chapel in order to exorcize the demons in residence.

I kid you not.

That's a true story.

Such activity did not bode well with many at our school, including a large number of our faculty. After all, how could we not take offence at the idea that our chapel, where services were dedicated to the praise of the triune God, was host to a legion of demons? The very idea that our holy space harbored fallen angels was an affront to many within our school. For me, however, it was a time of great excitement. Whatever was going to happen, it was bound to be interesting.

And interesting it was. During the first service one of the evangelist's intercessors sat in the front row chanting "Jesus, Jesus, Jesus." He did this the entire time.

I mean, the entire time.

As he did, I tried to keep count, but I couldn't keep up. It wounded my brain to even try. One funny thing did come out of it though: a friend of mine, an older religion major whose focus was the Hebrew Bible, had the good sense to follow up with an occasional, "Moses, Moses, Moses."

Who said Nazarenes were bereft of humor?

We were later told that the recitation of "Jesus, Jesus, Jesus" was this person's mantra meant to keep the evangelist safe from demonic intervention.

"I thought they already prayed the demons out of here?" I queried.

One of my professors, who I knew secretly thought this all a pompous show, looked at me as if to say, "Tripp, you're not helping things."

We were informed by his intercessory crew that this particular evangelist was so in tune with the workings of the Holy Spirit that he was often a primary target for demonic attack.

I know, that just doesn't make sense, right? Though it did make me sort of glad to be a half-ass Christian. If getting close to God makes you more susceptible to Satan's all-out arsenal, I think I will keep my distance (of course, here I am now trying to get a closer look, so take that as you will).

Apparently, this revivalist was sort of like a religious Dean and Sam Winchester. You know those guys from the television show *Supernatural*? They go around hunting demons, ghosts, and all sorts of angry spirits in order to save the bodies and souls of their fellow humans. Instead of using shotguns filled with salt and Latin incantations, this evangelist spent most of his time preaching out of the Gospel of Matthew (chosen due to its large number of references to demons), and having his crew say Jesus' name over and over and over again.

"How many times do you have to say the name 'Jesus' before they leave? Is there a magical number that you have to hit before they listen to you?" I asked.

Despite a number of my friends finding my questions humorous (though that was not my intention, I truly was seeking clarification), our guests were not quite as pleased with the sacrilege coming out of my mouth.

Before they could scold me, I quickly added, "Plus, I thought the battle had already been won."

"It has been won," stated one of his spiritual warfare henchmen. "But Satan is like a chicken with its head cut off. It still flaps its wings around the yard with the ability to hurt others with its thrashing talons, not even knowing it's doomed."

Satan is like a decapitated chicken with thrashing talons.

You just can't make that stuff up.

As entertaining as I found the entire situation to be, it created, for others, a profound impulse to look for Satan under every rock. During the following weeks I heard students blame everything on God's fallen angel:

- "My car won't start." Must be Satan.
- "Cafeteria food here sucks." Must be Satan.
- "Someone placed two big blue beach balls on top of the chapel under the steeple." Must be Satan. (Actually, I have another theory as to the culprit.)
- "My boyfriend wants to have premarital sex." Must be Satan.
- "My girlfriend doesn't want to have premarital sex." Must be Satan.

Well, maybe not that last one, but you get the picture. Satan gets the blame for everything. Now, I am not trying to say that if there really is an ontological personality known as Satan that this being is not responsible for some horrid things. But using Satan as an explanation for everything you personally do not like is not only theologically problematic, it is also terribly dangerous. It opens the door to the rampant demonization of other people despite Christianity's claim that all humans, regardless of creed, race, nationality, gender, or faith tradition (or, lack thereof), are created in the image of God.

And yes, even evolutionists bear the *imago Dei*.

SATAN GIVES BIRTH ON THE GALAPAGOS ISLANDS (AND KIRK CAMERON GOES BANANAS)

To say that the banana happened by accident is even more unintelligent than to say that no one designed the Coca Cola can.

—Kirk Cameron

Evolution is a bankrupt speculative philosophy, not a scientific fact. Only a spiritually bankrupt society could ever believe it. Only atheists could accept this Satanic theory.

—Jimmy Swaggart

Normally, I do not take too seriously the words of actors who do not understand the process of cultivating edible fruit, or the words of televangelists who have sex with prostitutes and threaten to kill homosexuals. Yet, their commentary is fairly indicative of those within Christianity who believe evolution undermines the biblical narrative. Equating the teachings of Darwin with that of a sinister master-plan of Satan is by no means novel or rare. For many Christians, it is simply not enough to disbelieve in evolution; one has the moral obligation to oppose it.

What evolution has to do with my search for Satan was not immediately obvious to me; only later did it become apparent. Though this book records the results of my plan to find Lucifer—or as he is more fondly known, Old Horny[4]—there were some conversations and situations that I merely stumbled into. What follows is one of these. I am including it because I find it such a compelling case for what it means to be defined, specifically, by what one opposes, and how this creates a tendency in us to demonize others in a manner that is rather, well, demonic.

So, here you go.

"Darwin was of the Devil!" screamed the African-American preacher. "He wants you to think that you came from apes! From monkeys! And now they want to teach that garbage, that lie of Satan, to our children. I say 'no!'"

And the people gathered cried out in one voice "No!"

"I say 'no' to those . . . those atheists, those . . . those God-deniers who want to tell our children we came from monkeys. I also say 'woe!'"

And the congregation screamed "woe!"

"I say woe to those who would pervert God's image, who would attempt to teach our children, even our adults . . ." As he slowly uttered those last three words his expression began to change. It was as if he was about to do battle for the very souls of the people he loves.

"Don't lie now, don't you dare lie. Some of you even right now at this very moment are thinking that science has all the answers, aren't ya'll?"

---

4. The Bible includes various names and titles for Satan: Abaddon, accuser, adversary, Apollyon, Beelzebul, Belial, deceiver of the world, Devil, dragon, evil one, father of lies, god of this world, liar, murderer, ruler of the demons, ruler of this world, and serpent of old. There are other common names associated with Satan including Lucifer, Mephistopheles, and the Prince of Darkness. For a real good time, however, call the Devil by some of his medieval names: Old Horny, Old Hairy, Gentleman Jack, The Good Fellow, Black Bogey, Old Scratch, and my personal favorite, Lusty Dick.

A conflagration of voices simultaneously filled the air: "Lord no!" "Heavens please forgive us if we did!" "No, no, no good reverend, no!" "I love the lord!" "Sweet Jesus save us!"

It was an overwhelming experience. So chaotic, yet so controlled.

"That's the Holy Spirit working," I was later told.

The reverend's smile returned when he found the response he wanted to hear. "I know, I know ya'll are some God-fearing, God-loving people. And I know none of ya, not a one of ya, would ever betray their Lord for anyone who would try to tell you that you descended from a monkey. Of all the absurd, irrational, atheistic God-hating things I have ever heard. Do you honestly think you would have had your freedom if you weren't created in the image of God?"

"Oh, save us Jesus!" shouted a thin, elderly lady in the front row. Her hat must have weighed more than her body. It was huge. Big and white with various artificial flowers sprouting out of it. She started stomping her feet at the thought of her hard-fought battle for freedom. I'm guessing she was probably in her late sixties or early seventies. I thought about how she had probably seen her fair share of evil.

"Jesus has saved you Audrey! Praise him right now!" exclaimed their preacher. Not that Audrey needed an invitation, but with it she threw down moves that would have impressed the most devout fan of "Saturday Night Fever."

It was truly a sight to behold.

Amidst the blaring music and harmonization of voices, Audrey was dancing like nobody's business. It made me think of the victory dance King David might have given when he danced through the streets of his kingdom, except there were no jealous people to condemn her for her doxological body.

People were shedding their coats, tossing their hats, stomping their feet, clapping their hands, singing in shouts, shouting in song, and all the while, sitting in the very back, was a lone white boy starting to understand what Du Bois meant by his narration of practicing double-consciousness.

I was thinking many things, but at that particular point I was thinking about what seemed to be an interesting leap of logic. To suggest that Darwin's teaching could undermine the further advancement of civil rights was something new to me. If this service ever ends, I was thinking, I'll ask him about it.

Several exhilarating, yet very exhausting, hours later, I finally landed the chance to chat with the minister.

I explained to him that I really enjoyed their service. To be sure, this was not your typical Sunday service. It wasn't even on a Sunday; it was on a Friday night. The service was also not held in a church, but in a theater. I was working part-time as the Assistant Technical Director at the Paramount Theater in Burlington, North Carolina. Since the theater is owned by the city, it can be rented by anyone for any occasion. Interestingly enough, we have as many church groups rent the theater as local acting communities. It holds about four hundred people, and you have plenty of stage space for your performers. It also has all sorts of perks that many church groups find advantageous. Therefore, it is often rented for staged dramas, revivals, Southern Gospel concerts, weddings, and the occasional ecclesial variety show. This particular event was a combination of a relatively improvised play followed by a very lengthy worship service.

"I don't care if they call this place a theater," shouted the minister, "right now it's the house of God!"

I cannot tell you how many different ministers have used that same line. It's as if they feel the need to apologize for having a church service in a "godless" theater, so they decide to reclaim it for Christ—even if only for a few hours.

After it was over, I helped with the load out, took care of all my technical duties, and asked the minister for a few moments of his time. He was more than happy to speak with me. I introduced myself as a student, and teacher, of theater and theology, and that I was interested in asking him a few questions about Satan. Of course, like any good conversation you need to get the introductions down correctly. I wasn't sure of his exact title (a number of people referred to him with different designations), so I asked what he wanted to be called.

"You can call me the Lord's Servant, a vessel for his voice, a preacher called and sent and thus proudly went—wherever the good Lord tells me to go. Or, you can just call me Reverend Irving, Mr. Brother Tripp. Or, should I call you Doctor? Doctor Tripp?"

"Oh no, that's not necessary. I only require my students and enemies to refer to me with that appellation. Actually, I'm kind of fond of Brother Tripp. Makes me feel like we're in this together."

"Ha, ha! Now that is what I'm talking about. Yes sir, we are in this together. All the way, now and in the here-after. I like that. I don't even know you, Brother Tripp, but you and me, we're in this together, and do you know why?"

Taking my best guess I offered, "Jesus?"

"Praise his holy name. I can talk to you, Brother Tripp. And I like someone I can talk to. You know what I'm saying?"

"Yes sir, I believe I do."

"That's good. That's good."

Despite his participation in a play, his hour long homily, and his leading of the congregation in a dozen or so songs, my new brother-in-arms, Reverend Irving, had plenty of energy left for conversation. You have to admire that sort of drive.

Immediately after the introductions, I told him what I wished to discuss and thanked him, in advance, for honoring my odd request of subject matter.

"Talking about Satan?" he asked. "That's not odd. We talk about Satan all the time. You better talk about Satan. The moment you let your guard down is the moment he will conform you to his ways."

"Well, that's kind of what I want to talk to you about. Satan's ability to conform us to his ways, as you suggest. So . . ." I intuited his desire to cut in. "Yes?"

"No, go ahead."

"No, no, please," I told him. "I'm here to ask you questions. I want to hear what you have to say, so any time you feel like saying something, please jump in."

"Let me ask you something, Brother Tripp, if you don't mind."

"Not at all. Please."

"Why do you think you are here wanting to talk to me about Satan?" he asked. "Now think seriously about that for a moment. Why are you here, on this very night, talking to me?"

"Well, to be honest—"

"I wouldn't have it any other way," he interrupted.

"Ha-ha. Of course. Well, there are any number of contingencies that enable us to find ourselves in certain places with certain people at certain times. I guess in this situation the fact that I work here may be the most obvious reason."

I could tell he was not satisfied with my response, so he offered another possibility. "But you don't think this was some sort of accident, do you?"

As I stood there trying to find the right words I sensed he already had the answer he wanted to hear, but he was kind enough to allow me the opportunity to figure it out for myself.

"No, by contingencies," I continued, "I'm not referring to an accident per se, just the idea that I could have very easily ended up somewhere else tonight, or you could have been somewhere else, or—"

"Right, right," he interrupted. "Now think about that for a second. You could be anywhere else in this world having this conversation, or not having this conversation, yet here we are, together, talking about the one responsible for the fall of all creation. Why do you think that is?"

"I'm guessing you think it's by design?"

"As is all things," he furtively grinned. "Now, I want you to think about that before we go any further."

After standing there quietly feigning thought for a moment or so I asked him, "Are you suggesting that I was meant to be here? That God led me to this particular moment?"

Laughing rather loudly, almost beside himself, he said, "I'm not suggesting it, Brother Tripp, I am saying it! Praise the Lord! Come on with me now. Praise his holy name!"

I stood there looking at him a bit confused.

"Oh, uh, you mean right now?"

"Right now! Praise his name, Brother Tripp, praise it!"

"Okay . . . praise Jesus," I softly offered.

Being none too pleased with my pitiful attempt, he said, "Come on now; say it like you mean it!"

"Well, I do mean it." Now it was my turn to preach. "But I think one of the problems of contemporary Christianity is it confines praise of God to what we do with our voices, when praise of God occurs through acts of charity, the enactment of justice, obedience to Jesus. You know, St. Francis said to preach the Gospel everyday, and if you have to, use words. I think that is a—"

"I love that, Brother Tripp, I love that!" he interrupted excitedly. "I'm going to use that sometime, but right now I need you to praise his name for me!"

"For you?"

"No, no, not for me. Not even for Jesus, but for you."

"Well, that could be a bit Feuerbachian, but, at the same time I guess—" and before I could finish my sentence he shouted at the top of his lungs, "PRAISE HIS HOLY NAME, BROTHER TRIPP!"

"PRAISE JESUS!" I screamed in terror.

"That's right, that's right," he said, bringing it back down to a civilized decibel. "Praise the Lord."

"Yes sir."

"How do you feel about that?" he proudly asked.

"A bit high strung. Maybe a little frightened. My heart is beating pretty hard, but, uh, overall, pretty good."

"Ha-ha, yes sir, yes sir. That heart is beating hard because Jesus is in it. And now we know why you're here, don't we?" he asked with a very pleased tone.

"I think so," I told him. "I really do, and that is, in a very round about way, what I want to talk about. This conversation about Satan, it's really about a pursuit of God, or as you just, I think, eloquently suggested, God's pursuit of us."

"That's right."

"Well, and, I'm not completely sure how I want to begin this conversation, but I guess, in a way, during the service you sort of gave me a lead on how, perhaps, this conversation could go."

"It's funny how things work out that way, isn't it, Brother Tripp? It wouldn't be a mere coincidence, now would it?"

"I'm guessing you're thinking 'no.'"

"That's right," he confirmed.

"So, earlier in the service you were talking about science, and presumably, at least specifically, from what I gather, the claims of evolutionary biology that suggest we share a common ancestor with other primates. And then you made an interesting—"

"Well, now hold on there a second," he interrupted. "What do you mean by 'other primates'?"

"Oh, well, only that homo-sapiens, based on a number of anatomical characteristics, maybe the similarities in our DNA, something about opposable thumbs, I don't really know as I'm not a zoologist, but based on whatever sort of taxonomy of characteristics we are classified as a primate."

"According to . . . ?" he slowly asked.

"Um, well, people. Scientists."

"Let me ask you something, Brother Tripp. Why is *that* the standard of truth? Why is the model of science held as the ultimate bearer of truth? Especially when we know, you and I that is, when we know that Jesus is the truth. Are you suggesting that Jesus was a monkey?"

That question is as funny today as it was then. Seriously, go back and re-read it. Take your time. It's hilarious. I'm not going anywhere. Re-read it. He actually asked me if I thought Jesus was a monkey. I wanted to say, "No sir. I learned in my first year of divinity school that Jesus was human. Once we figured out Jesus wasn't a monkey, why the complexities of pneumatology, the Trinity, and the hypostatic union just fell right into place."

Just for fun, though, can you imagine if Jesus had been a monkey? Imagine the manifestation of the Second Person of the triune God as a capuchin or a red howler. Insanity would ensue. What a time we would be having, what a time! Regardless, his question caught me completely off guard and I exploded into laughter. I mean, uncontrollable laughter. I couldn't stop until I realized, through my teary eyes, that he wasn't laughing with me.

"Um, no sir, not at all," I muttered as I was trying to pretend like I was coughing and not laughing. "Again, one can be a primate and not be a monkey. And historically I don't think the church has had much of a problem referring to humans as animals, or being classified along with other animals as such. Indeed, that is something we share in common, as the Noahic covenant suggests, with all those creatures that God created."

"Exactly. And atheist scientists want to pervert that by referring to humans, the one creature on this earth made in God's holy image, as descending from monkeys and gorillas. Now," he asked, "how do you square those two?"

"Well, first of all," I responded, still trying to choke away the tears, "I don't think anyone is actually suggesting that humans descended from monkeys. The claim is that monkeys, apes, chimps, tamarins, and others, along with humans, may share a common ancestor. I think that is the claim, and it is being made not just by scientists who happen to be atheists, but by scientists who are Jewish, Christian, Muslim, Hindu. As a matter of fact, in 1996 Pope John Paul II—"

Cutting me off, again, he said, "That makes it even worse. When God's very own people neglect Scripture for secular scientific theories, and that's all these things are—theories created by the Devil to fool us into thinking we're no better than monkeys."

(An important aside: What does everybody have against monkeys? Has anyone actually paid any attention to them? They're awesome. If only we were so cool.)

I spent a few moments trying to explain that a theory in science is not to be confused for a wild guess or mere speculation. I told him that a lot of conclusive evidence goes into making a theory a theory, and that it takes a lot of work just to get to the point of being able to call something a theory. I also told him there are a number of theories that many of us seem to take for granted: cell theory, theory of special relativity and general relativity, as well as gravitational theory. I was trying to explain that evolution would not be a theory if it were not thought to be on par with the evidence that makes any of these theories, well, theories. Realizing this was not going anywhere, I decided to get to the more important point he made about the connection between evolution and Satan.

"You just stated that the Devil created or influenced, I guess you might say, the theory of evolution. Out of curiosity," I asked, "how would you know that? I don't mean to be antagonistic, I'm genuinely curious. How do you know that the Devil is behind the formation of certain scientific theories?"

"It's easy Brother Tripp. Jesus says that you are either with him or against him. There is no in-between. That's Matthew 12:30. Is this not correct? Am I not understanding him correctly?"

"I don't know if that specific passage is saying—"

"It's Matthew 12:30," he reiterated.

"Okay, yeah, I believe you. I'm familiar with the text. I think it is actually repeated in both Mark and Luke, though I'm not sure—"

"Exactly. Therefore, any teaching, or anything for that matter, that conflicts with the truth that is Jesus is against him, and, therefore, comes from the Devil. The Devil is the father of all lies, Brother Tripp. That's the Gospel of John 8:44: 'Whenever he speaks a lie, he speaks from his own nature; for he is a liar, and the father of lies.' That, Brother Tripp, is how I know these things, and that's how you can know them, too."

"Okay, so, in your understanding Darwin was demonic, or, at least greatly influenced by the Devil?"

"As with anyone who follows his teachings."

"But how does this happen?" I asked. "I mean, I know numerous people that are Christian, Jewish, and folks of no religious persuasion whatsoever, who are Darwinian in terms of how they understand the development of the human race. Your claim that these people are demonic is rather inhospitable, to say the least. I think it's a great affront to Christian sensibilities to label another person, whom we believe to be created in the image of God, with this sort of blanket demonic generalization just because they think differently from you on the processes that occur for life to get from one stage to the next."

"It is a very serious matter indeed, but would you not say that Hitler and the German people were under his influence?"

Wow. I love the leaps.

"Wait, under whose influence?" I asked. "Darwin or the Devil?"

"Both."

"Well, there is no doubt that German Christianity co-opted with National Socialism, and blind allegiance to their tribal god, was certainly a principality and power that—"

"Was under the direct control of Satan! Amen?"[5]

"Absolutely," I agreed. "The Holocaust is clearly the failure of Christianity especially as it wed itself to German nationalism underwritten by Enlightenment-based ideologies. I think I am quite good with that claim. If there was ever a moment of wholesale demonic possession of a people, I think that is a pretty classic example. As a matter of fact I have written extensively, in particular, on nation-states as those principalities and powers that tempt us to give allegiance to them that, in this case, made possible something like Nazi Germany and—"

"And are therefore demonic. Amen?"

I was beginning to question whether or not I was even required for our conversation. He kept cutting me off.

He, of course, continued, "Just as Satan uses kings and presidents, and all sorts of power to do his bidding, why would Satan not also use scientists, or engineers, or whomever to lead people even further away from God? People need to be told when they have succumbed to the influence of all those powers at odds with the Lord. And how else will they know if we don't tell him? You're an educated man. You know Scripture. You know all about Isaiah, Jeremiah, Micah, Amos, and Hosea."

"Hosea was married to a whore," I said with the authority of one being ignored.

He didn't blink an eye.

"You know it was their job," he continued, "their task, a task they did not even want, to tell people the word that they didn't always want to hear. And that's all I'm doing now. That's what you saw me do tonight. I'm being a prophet, and prophets are rarely liked by the people they are commanded to prophesy to. You have a whole Bible full of examples. I

---

5. I envy any person untroubled by the world of nuance.

just named some of them. Jeremiah wept at what he had to do. Isaiah was probably killed for it. You think Hosea wanted to marry Gomer?"

I guess he did hear me.

"Nobody," he continued, "wanted to hear the word they spoke, but that didn't keep them from speaking it. And I'm telling you now, anyone who thinks we come from monkeys, or shares a common ancestor, as you say, with monkeys, is a liar. And Jesus said that all liars are of the Devil. Why? Because the Devil is a liar. But you already know this. 'There is no truth in him,' says the Gospel of John. 'There is no truth in him.'"

"So, just to be clear," I interjected, "because I want to make sure I am totally understanding you on this—let's not leave anything to a possible misunderstanding—are you suggesting that just as Hitler and those that followed his lead were under the influence of Satan, so too are those that believe in evolution?"

"Now, Brother Tripp, you know I don't suggest anything."

"Ah, that's right, that's right. You're saying it?"

"Praise the Lord."

"Of course."

At this point, we talked a little more about natural selection, Hitler's use of social Darwinism, and basically all the usual things that come out of a conversation such as ours. He never grew impatient with me, or tired of my questions, even when he could tell I was rather appalled, to say the least, by some of his insinuations. It was never clear to me why believing that life evolves somehow necessarily conflicts with the teachings of Jesus, but, alas, he was never convinced of how the two did not conflict. We reached an impasse, but not before one last question.

A question for me.

"Brother Tripp, do you believe in evolution?"

Knowing this could only go in one direction, I tried to offer an answer that would end up with him not thinking I was demonic, but was still truthful. "Well, it's sort of a pointless question. I mean, my beliefs, or yours for that matter, in no way have any bearing on whether or not life evolves, so I—"

"Brother Tripp, do you believe in evolution?"

Biting the bullet I responded, "Yes sir. I think we have more than enough conclusive evidence that life evolves and it continues to evolve. We can see it in laboratories, we can trace it in—"

"I'll pray for you, Brother Tripp. I will pray for you."

"To . . . wait, hold on a second," his declaration of prayer for me threw me off a bit. "Are you going to pray that I no longer believe in the claims made by the vast majority of all people who have spent their entire lives in the field of the natural sciences? That I no longer believe in evolution?"

"Brother Tripp, you sought me out so that you could ask me some questions about Satan. Hopefully what you have learned today is that, sometimes," and he leaned into me making sure I didn't mistake the meaning of these next words, "you don't have to look very far to find what you're looking for."

Ouch.

I mean, really, ouch.

Well, at least he doesn't pull punches.

My kind of guy.

I couldn't ask for a better ending to our conversation. Truth be told, he may be on to something. Sometimes what we are looking for is right in front of us, or, in regards to Satan, perhaps inside of us. The thing is, I don't feel particularly possessed. No red glowing eyes or wicked thoughts—save for those against the University of North Carolina Tarheels basketball program. Yet, the good reverend is going to pray that I will be delivered from the power of the natural sciences.

That, if nothing else, is certainly interesting.

2 DEFYING THE DEVIL

Satan's successes are the greatest when he appears
with the name of God on his lips.
—Mahatma Gandhi

The lunatic, the lover, and the poet
Are of imagination all compact:
One sees more devils than vast hell can hold;

—Theseus
(William Shakespeare, *A Midsummer Night's Dream*)

"There is not a day that goes by that I couldn't call you and give you another story," confessed a pastor of a small church in Alabama. After I told him about my research, he started calling me every time he had a new story about how Satan was attempting, according to his parishioners, to thwart their daily plans.

"If I could just get them to believe that God was as much at work as Satan," he lamented, "I would have a pretty good church."

Yet, this is also not without its problems. For instance, he informed me that during the Winter Olympics one of his parishioners, an elderly lady who had been in the church her whole life, called him to confess how torn she was between doing her daily devotions and watching figure skating.

"Satan just didn't want me to do my devotions," she told him. "Instead, he tried to convince me that watching figure skating was not that big of a deal. I must confess to you pastor, I was really tempted, just this one time, to not do my daily Bible study. But do you know what happened? Jesus melted that ice just enough that they had to postpone the event. He knew I was struggling with what Satan was offering me, and so when I needed Jesus the most, He came through for me."

Does that mean Jesus is behind global warming?

What is interesting about this story is how this lady imagined God and Satan doing battle over her daily activities. Granted, this is hardly a new phenomenon. The early church claimed that God and Satan were locked in battle over their embodied souls. That is why the early church talked so much about the presence of both God and Satan—especially as it revolved around the issue of martyrdom. Throughout the vast majority of martyrdom accounts, many within the church imagined the Roman Arena—that space where Christians were fed to lions, or burned at the stake, or killed by gladiators—to be the arena where God and Satan displayed their cosmic battle. For the early Christians, dying a good death in the arena, dying as a witness to Christ, was an example of God's power over evil.[1] Now, however, God melts ice in order to trump Satan's nefarious plans.

For many Christians, God and Satan are active in every aspect of their daily lives. There is no room for chance, luck, accidents, the forces of nature, or contingency; we are simply at the center of a long-standing battle between the God of creation and the god of the earth—which, you would think, would make the locating of at least one of these combatants relatively easy. In order to better my chances of finding the one keeping elderly ladies from their devotions, I decided to pursue a group of Christian warriors who claimed to battle the Devil on a daily basis. Perhaps they would be able to shed some light on this journey.

FAITH FORCE: "EXERCISING" DEMONS

How can one enter a strong man's house and plunder his property, without first tying up the strong man? Then indeed the house can be plundered.

—Jesus (Matt 12:29)

"Sometimes," exclaimed a very large man carrying a telephone pole, "you just have to show Satan some muscle."

---

1. See for instance my book, *The Purple Crown*.

"And when God is on your side, who can be against you?" asked another who was tearing through a phone book.

The brute strength of these guys was impressive. They were punching through cinderblocks, tying horseshoes into knots, and breaking baseball bats against their backs and legs all in an effort to bring people to Christ. Despite the fact that Christianity is a religion that elevates the weak, the powerless, the poor, and the lowly, here was a display of faith in which all of the participants were in top physical shape (granted, there could be a number of joint issues in their futures). These warriors were accomplishing feats of physicality only ever found in comic books.

Being a sucker for a good comic book, it captured my interest.

I was mostly intrigued, however, to find out where anyone would get the idea to use physical strength as a means of bringing people to know a nonviolent Jew from the first century. After all, there has to be some connection between the means of our witness and that which is being witnessed to. Just how does one come up with the idea of putting on spandex and bench-pressing their way to God? What kind of people would be interested in such a scenario?

"People, especially in the West, are mystified with the idea of the stellar athlete, the strong man, the whole superhero mentality," one of the members of Faith Force told me. "We simply capitalize on this fascination; we use it as a catalyst to bring others to the saving knowledge of Jesus Christ."

Frank is a bodybuilder, a gym owner, a member of a group called Faith Force, and, more importantly, "a man saved by God in August of 1991 at a revival in a basketball gym." He told me that at the time he had taken every body-enhancing drug on, behind, and under the market. This goes well beyond the normal cycling of popular anabolic steroids; instead, let your mind roam around horse and monkey hormones and you will get an idea as to what bodybuilders in the eighties were willing to try in order to procure the ultimate pump. He had injected all sorts of things in his body in order to make it simultaneously bigger *and* leaner. Now, however, he is a Christian. His body is a temple of the Holy Spirit. Steroids will no longer be a part of his life as they are destructive to the flesh that houses the Spirit of God.

Frank, however, didn't leave bodybuilding; he only left the illegal aspects of it. Since the mid-nineties, he has become a minister of sorts, and his ministry has been an unusual one. It includes witnessing to those men and women who spend much of their time building muscle mass while reducing their body fat. He has found his niche. He has taken a once struggling gym (one that does not offer all of the sparkling amenities found in the quick-fix gyms popping up all over this body-obsessed culture) and has used it as a vehicle for ministering to those in search of something more than just the physical. Although you do not have to be a Christian to train in his gym, you should not be surprised to hear Jars of Clay, Switchfoot, Haste the Day (yeah, metal-core) or any other Christian rock band blaring out of the speakers while you're hammering away at squats.

"It gets your mind on God," a gym member informed me, "so you can lose yourself in what you're doing. I think it makes you stronger." Granted, this particular guy had the military press machine loaded with five or six forty-five pound plates, so he may be on to something. Then again, it could have something to do with his 5,000 plus calorie a day diet that includes an excessive amount of protein shakes.

It could be a little of both.

I asked Frank, a man I have had the good fortune to know for a long time, if he thought that the mystification with the superhero was a positive thing.

"Not necessarily," he told me, "as it does glorify the strong often times at the expense of those who are weak."

I wanted to ask him why he would even bother feeding this mentality. Why not subvert it with an image that is more in line with the gospel, for example, with the witness of Mother Theresa or Dorothy Day? These were two women who certainly were strong, but not in the sense of how the powerful tend to understand strength. This emphasis on physical strength seems to, ironically, confirm Nietzsche's claim that Christianity subverts the natural order of things by elevating the weak and the ignoble. These guys were trying to prove Nietzsche wrong by showing how strong and tough Christians can be. At least, so I thought. Before I could ask my question, he seemed to anticipate my thoughts and immediately jumped in:

"Look, we use our physical strength to set up that sort of conversation. Scripture is very clear that we are in a battle not with flesh and blood, but are locked in a spiritual battle with principalities and powers. The size or strength of a person is irrelevant to their maturity in faith. What we do is display our physical strength in order to capitalize on our point that nothing we can do physically can save us. Despite our ability to do all these things that impress our audience, the strong man cannot free himself. All of us lack the strength to free ourselves from our personal captivities. Since the fall of humanity, authority has been given over to Satan to tempt us to rely on ourselves in all things. So, we impress these people with our physical abilities, yet we quickly let them know that despite our physical strength, we are helpless against the one who would tear us down without the blood of Jesus. When people see such a display of strength yet recognize that this does nothing against the spiritual battle for our very souls, they come to realize that it is only Jesus in us that makes us truly strong."

Frank had clearly thought this through and seemed to revel in the paradoxical nature of Faith Force. Their strength actually revealed their weaknesses, and this is what they were attempting to highlight.

"So," I asked, "you think that such a performance enables people to better listen to the message of Christianity?"

"I run a fitness center, and most of the time with the nature of this business it is all about us, everything about our appearance, our abilities, our strengths, our accolades. When it comes to Christianity, it points us to our faith in Christ and his resurrection. In any business, you don't talk religion and you don't talk politics, so we use the catalyst of our strength which gives us the opportunity to break this taboo. And because we believe it is a spiritual issue, that is, you can't intellectualize Christianity or faith, the testimony of our team is based on our spiritual effort."

This was a fascinating response. One cannot intellectualize Christianity, that is, one cannot be too dependent upon the brain for it, yet, we can bear witness to its truths through other body parts like the forearms, triceps, trapezoids, etc., in order to, oddly enough, combat an essentially spiritual issue. Given my fondness for the writings of Søren Kierkegaard, I admit to enjoying a good paradox.

He explained that the main theme of Faith Force was to commit feats of incredible strength in light of the text "the strong man cannot free himself." Regardless of their level of strength, their testimony was that they did not have the power to free themselves from their personal vices.

"Some of these guys," he explained, "were bound for suicide, bound to drugs, and our culture does not allow us to appear weak, and our testimony is that we are the weakest of all, despite this show of strength."

"In Faith Force," he continued, "and I hear everything through the filter of Scripture, it says you are not dealing with flesh and blood, we are dealing with principalities and powers. I believe when the fall of man came, the original authority meant for man was given to Satan. As a Pentecostal believer, to make Jesus Lord we break the ability of Satan over our lives. I see it in the gym, because I do believe there is a devil in every situation. You are either going to serve God or serve the world, and Satan has total reign to do whatever Satan wants in the lives of those without Christ. It's the largest power in heaven next to God. But, as a Pentecostal believer, I believe in the power of the blood to break that demonic power in the lives of people."

I asked him if he would say more about the omnipresent status and influence of Satan. I needed him to be very specific as to how he understood his rule. "For instance," I asked him, "based on what you just said— that is, you are either going to serve God or the world—would you say that everyone that does not confess Christ is under the power or influence of Satan?

With no hesitation he said, "I absolutely believe so."

"So," I asked, "even if it is a Gandhi, Aung San Suu Kyi, or any faithful adherent of any of the world's religions, you would still say that they are under the authority of Satan?"

"I don't think Satan ever tells a complete lie, he just never tells the whole truth."

"That is, actually, a very interesting point" (as well as an admirable deflection) "I wonder—"

"Humanism," he interrupted, "and great people have done great things, but, listen, 'no one comes to the Father but through me,' and because I look at the Bible solely, and I can see a snapshot of the future coming, there is going to be a terrible rebellion against Christianity because true Christianity is never tolerated."

"Well, on that latter part, I agree," I said. "I think those who follow the path of Jesus are often as despised by other Christians as they are by the so-called 'world.' Whether it is the Berrigan Brothers, Oscar Romero, or Dorothy Day, their actions kept them in trouble with both the church and the state."

"But, you cannot get to God without going through Jesus."

Another classic deflection. I could learn from this guy.

Continuing, he said, "And without the shedding of blood there is no forgiveness of sins, and you can intellectualize and see the great works by men, but if we are truly dealing with spiritual issues, I believe there is a booger in the closet, and it will always come back. Great men came up with medicine and now we have a situation in which the tack is in our backsides and we don't know how to remove it, so we give them medicine so they forget its there."

I have to be honest, I wasn't 100 percent sure what he was talking about. I wasn't even 50 percent sure, so I tried backing up a step.

"Let's go back for a second, because I'm captivated by this notion of being either under the power of God or under the power of Satan with no in-between. I think it is Luke in the Book of Acts who talks about Cornelius being a God-fearer prior to the gospel coming to him. Do you think that God's grace extends beyond the cultural ethos that Christianity has touched? I mean, if you are born in certain parts of India then there is a very large chance that you are going to be a Hindu. Or, if you are born in Thailand you are going to be a Buddhist. Then you have the case of Job, who is neither Jewish nor, obviously, Christian, so, do you think there is still room for God's grace to be active in a place where Christianity does not exist, or even where Christianity, despite itself, does exist? And I don't think such a question necessarily needs to take anything away from the manifestation of God in Jesus."

"Absolutely," he responded, "every Muslim, Hindu, and Nigerian will have the opportunity to accept or reject Christ, and his coming back and judgment will not occur until this is a possibility.[2] And now technology is such that within the next ten years there will not be a place on this planet where a person will not have had the opportunity to hear the gospel."

You hear that Jacques Ellus, Neil Postman, and the rest of you Luddites? Technology is not only a good, but it will bring about the Second Coming!

"It doesn't matter," he continued, "if it is a Hindu or a homosexual, it all comes to the Spirit, and when man meets the truth of God, the real truth, the question is not whether they are Hindu, Muslim, or homosexual, but what are you going to do with this truth?"

How much more interesting would world religions courses be if we could count homosexuality as one of the world's leading religions? Huston Smith, it looks like it's time for a new edition.

2. Is there such a thing as Nigerianism? Is that a religion? If so, I can see the academics scurrying to write yet another book of zero interest to anyone beyond the reach of the AAR. Of course, selling only a few hundred copies of a book never stopped anyone from getting an endowed chair. Yep, the academy is a sham. Keep sending your children and money to us, please.

"Well," I suggested, "let's talk specifics about Satan. Granted, the Pentecostal Church, as with my original church home, the Nazarenes, at least in the Southeast, cannot seem to get enough of Satan. By that I mean, it was always a subject of concern. I personally always thought—at least not as a child, as I was quite terrified of Satan—that if Satan *is* at work, then Satan would be wiser working the subtleties."

"Yes, yes."

"So, you agree?"

"Oh, yes, but it takes many forms, and believe me it's true, it's very real."

"Well, that is the heart of the matter for me. The reality of it all. Have you ever seen any demons?"

His answer?

"I've talked to them."

Thank you Lord, we are now getting somewhere.

"It was in my gym, 8:30 AM on a Thursday," he explained. "It was on an old Sears treadmill. I had a new trainee and as she was on the treadmill the demons in her started talking to me."

"*While* she was on the treadmill?" I asked.

"Yes."

"Wow." Unable to resist, I had to say it, "Talk about *exercising* some demons. Ha-ha, get it? Exercising demons! Ha-ha-ha . . . ah . . . uh . . . yeah."

My pun was met with a very awkward silence.

Deciding it best to move on, I asked him, "What were the demons saying?"

"That the woman belonged to them; despite her desire to break free from them, she belonged to them. She had given her soul, her body, over to their dominion. I said, 'Young woman do you wish to be free?' She would try to say 'yes,' but the demons would shout over her, and I would have to rebuke them."

"There were numerous demons in her?"

"Yes."

"How did she get them?" I asked.

"Through witchcraft and their rituals. These people were engaged in astral projection, levitation, all sorts of black magic."

I asked for more details on what kind of witches he was talking about, because most of the witches I have encountered have been unabashedly harmless. They have been far more reminiscent of hippies running around in circles wanting to make love to river nymphs, talking about springing forth from the womb of Gaia, and casting spells in order to banish negative energy. They have always reminded me of what you would get if you crossed Norman Vincent Peale with Yoko Ono.

"There is no such thing as harmless witchcraft," he told me. "Whatever kind of witches and sorcerers these people were, they were heavily into the occult. I went with her to one of her groups in order to confront these demons, along with those controlling them, and as I was speaking to her, she was begging to be let go as they were painting pentagrams on the walls."

"Who was painting pentagrams on the walls?" I asked. "The demons?"

"No, no, the other people there. They were the ones painting pentagrams."

"While you were praying for her?"

"Yes, and through the pleading of the blood of Christ I commanded that the demons let her go, and they vacated her body."

"Where did they go?" I asked.

"Who?"

"The demons? Where did you send them? Where did they go?"

"To the place of outer darkness."

"Where is . . . I mean, how . . ." I had so many questions, I didn't know where to begin. "How did they get out of the outer darkness in the first place?"

"Through conjuration, black magic, satanic rituals."

"I'm so confused," I admitted. "So, Satan and his demons are all over this earth exercising authority over all who are not under the sacrificial blood of Christ, yet these demons still require our seeking them out of this outer darkness in order to be possessed?"

"There are levels of demonic possession," he answered. "And while those outside of Christ are under Satan's influence, due to her seeking of the dark forces she became a slave to them. I have always said that the most vicious fighters are scared fighters. They fight scared, but then they give themselves over to it. You open yourself up to it. Same way with the gym; you start out with baby weights and if you hang around long enough you become a big boy. So, when it comes to spiritual issues, people who surrender themselves to the occult, and there are no maybes here . . . we are talking about people who can speak to a bird in the air and it fall dead to the ground."

"Whoah."[3]

Before I could talk to him about how people can kill birds with their words, or what purpose such power would serve, or, what if they were in a town with bird sanctuary laws, he continued, "We think we are going to have them do our bidding, but we become enslaved to them, oppressed by them, chained to them, never to be let go without the power of Christ. The Bible says that 'Whom you give yourself over to, is whom you become a servant to.'"

With that, he started wrapping up the conversation. He wanted to let me know, in no uncertain terms, not to take this stuff lightly, nor to seek that which I think I could somehow handle. I hold no grand aspirations about controlling demons or anything of that nature; I just want to meet one in order to find out if there is anything beyond the phenomenal world that can be known to us through something other than vague feelings or rather often capricious beliefs. I understand that many people would argue that demons are of the spiritual world (or, perhaps, noumenal in the sense of true reality), yet, apparently, they have ability to materialize. I wish to be privy to such a materialization. Who knows, I could become the next John Constantine.

I duly appreciated the concern he revealed for me in this project. I have spoken with this man countless times about this subject, and I know that he is an honest person full of heartfelt conviction. He is a kind man, a gentle giant of sorts. His candid honesty about everything ranging from steroids, demons, and the proper form for bench pressing remains most welcome.

As with all second-hand stories, however, there are always questions that remain unanswered. Most notably, in this situation, if this woman was truly possessed by numerous demons, why was she in the gym doing cardio? Seriously. I have absolutely no idea what it means to be possessed by a demon, but I am hard-pressed to believe that if I were under the control of what was explained to me to be the "second most powerful force" on earth, which just happens to be evil, I would be concerned about cutting a few pounds. Surely she did not conjure the demons in hopes of decreasing her total body fat percentage. Granted, the idea of someone

3. Yeah, I said "whoah" in that way Keanu Reeves, in all of his movies, says "whoah."

in this culture striking such a bargain is not that far-fetched. There are Christian-based diet plans, so why not ask Satan for his tips on a healthy diet?

I'm not attempting to be facetious or sarcastic in regards to this situation. I'm taking it very seriously. It is, in fact, because I am taking it so seriously that I cannot help but ask these kinds of questions. Again, I'm not seeking to tear down, but simply to clarify. Something about it just doesn't make sense. Anytime we find people with demons in the Bible they are living in a graveyard, hanging out in a tree, or suffering from some physical deformity. I'm just a bit surprised that when demons took over this woman, she continued to feel the need to exercise. I'm not saying this because I think Frank was lying to me. I don't think that at all. Indeed, I think it is because he is telling me the truth, or at least how he interpreted the situation, that spawns such questions. This is crucial, as I'm just as interested in what people *consider* to be demonic possession as what could actually *be* demonic possession. This includes people's understanding of those who may be less obviously possessed than our woman on the treadmill with her verbose demons. By that I mean that if the vast number of Christians I have conversed with are correct, then people of other religious traditions, or who make certain arguments about the development of life, are also possessed. As pointed out by both Reverend Irving and the leader of Faith Force, anyone who does not consent to certain theological truths has no choice but to be under the power of Satan (and is that why they do not consent to certain theological truths, and, if so, is it really their fault?). Their demonically influenced lives may not be quite as dramatic as killing birds on verbal command, but it is, to quote the leader of Faith Force, "no less real." As popular exorcist Cindy Jacobs puts it, "There is a plot afoot, a serious threat to the nations of this Earth."[4]

Whether or not such a plot poses a threat to nations of planets other than Earth is yet to be discovered, but for now, we'll stick to this one.

---

4. Jacobs, *Deliver Us from Evil*, 70.

WHEN IN DOUBT, CAST IT OUT!
PMS, POVERTY, AND CINDY JACOBS' PUSSYCAT

*I, as a woman, have felt this spirit's presence [lust] manifest itself through
a man many times. . . . One of the primary ways you can know a spirit
of lust is at work is when you see a person's eyes sweep your whole body
the moment they come into contact with you. Of course, women can help
discourage the spirit of lust by carefully selecting what they wear.*

—Cindy Jacobs

Throughout the course of my research I read a large number of books on
spiritual warfare that agree with the sentiment that you are either under
the power of God or under the power of Satan. There is no in-between.
The good news is if you find yourself under the power of Satan, there are
numerous exorcists willing to lead you back to the path of glory. While I
will examine a very significant spiritual warrior in chapter 5, an important exorcist that I need briefly to mention at this point is Cindy Jacobs.

Cindy Jacobs is co-founder and president of Generals of Intercession
as well as an advocate of book burnings.[5] That latter detail may be some-
what important as her Website suggests she is a "respected prophet"
(which immediately distances herself from any of the prophets in the
Bible) who ministers not only to the common folk, but to "world influ-
encers who seek her prophetic advice." Due to her strong influence in the
world, she has also, she claims, been blessed by God by being honored
with two doctorates and has her own television show that she admits to
establishing as a counter to fortune-teller television shows.[6]

Jacobs is heavily involved with politics and can be seen on YouTube
performing mass exorcisms of demons that cause everything from poverty to homosexuality. She would no doubt agree with my friends in Faith
Force who find the presence of demons at work in everything that is "not

---

5. Ibid., 225. Book burnings are so environmentally unfriendly. Perhaps she could
discover a way to properly recycle all the material she finds problematic. Granted, I don't
care what she does with my books, as long as she pays for them first.

6. See online: www.generals.org/about-us/mike-cindy. If you go to their webpage you
can actually hear her husband talk about how busy they have been due to recent events.
He says, "We've been really, really busy because we keep having these things like oil spills
. . ." to which he is interrupted by Cindy's laughter. I have a pretty good sense of humor,
but I have yet to find the BP oil spill that funny.

under the protection of the blood of Christ." And by everything, I mean everything—including nonhuman animals.

While living in Texas, Jacobs heard her cat crying on her back porch, so she went to check on him. She said when she did, the cat "snarled, scratched and yowled like a banshee from hell. I definitely knew something other than our sweet pet was in that cat."[7]

At this point, she decided to call her husband for some spiritual backup. Her husband, Mike, was at a meeting, but this was too important to wait. She interrupted his meeting with a phone call, "Mike, will you come home as soon as you can? Our cat has a demon."

Cindy claims that being the "brilliant, analytical, Mr. Computer Brain sort in those days" he was, at first, a bit skeptical. (Does being skeptical of feline demonic possession really require such credentials?) Nevertheless, as soon as Mike got home and tried to touch the cat, he quickly agreed with his demon-sensitive wife. "Cindy, the cat does have a demon!" Cindy states, "I knew it was not politically correct to enjoy the moment too much, so I murmured, 'Perhaps we should take authority over it and set it free,' which we did. By the next morning, we had our affectionate little pet back."[8]

Cesar Milan, move over. There is a new pet whisperer in town.

This raises a few important theological questions: Everyone I have read on this subject, including Cindy Jacobs, argues that you have to, at some level, freely open yourself up to demonic possession in order to be possessed. Does this mean that cats can consciously choose whether or not to be possessed? And if so, what's in it for them?

A never-ending supply of catnip?

A tenth life?

A gold ball of yarn?

Boneless mice?

Does this also mean there is a whole world of Holy Ghost spirit-filled felines doing battle over the eternal prospect of their little kitty cat souls, or do they rely on us humans to exorcise their demons for them? Plus, if anything that is not under the protection of the blood of Christ is fair game for the Devil, does this mean we should baptize animals? (Given the sort of arguments we find for infant baptism, I don't see why

7. Ibid., 196.

8. Ibid.

not.) Also, and this is not really a theological question, but I wonder if the author has been around many other cats. I called my mother to ask her how many cats she thinks we had over my lifetime, and we guessed around thirty. That's a lot of cats. Then we figured up how many of those cats have bitten, scratched, or snarled at us and we came up with . . . yep, you guessed it, around thirty. Apparently, that's what cats do—even the ones we anthropomorphically designate as our "sweet pets."

Discovering that animals can be possessed by demons is not the only thing I learned from Cindy Jacobs. I also learned that if you are poor, struggle with PMS, have been named after a Catholic saint, or your husband is a religious/political leader who likes having sex with women other than you, then you are probably suffering from some sort of curse due to witches, your refusal to tithe, or your family's rich history of committing idolatry.

This was important for me to learn, and to include in this section of the book, for while the information I was gathering up to this point was suggesting evolutionists and non-Christians as the primary recipients of demonic possession, Jacobs also includes Christians as sufferers of the Devil's wiles. Jacobs complicates the matter by pointing out that what may look like a curse from Satan may actually be a curse from God.

The trick, it turns out, is discerning who is at work.

For instance, multiple times throughout her book she names poverty as a sign of disfavor with God (maybe that's why the Son had to die—Jesus was so damn poor he fell out of favor with the Father).[9] According to Jacobs, being poor is a sign that you or your family certainly did something to offend God. More than likely, your parents or grandparents were "God robbers."[10] That is, they didn't tithe. The quickest way to escape this curse is to pray for repentance and make sure you tithe appropriately. I'm sure you can probably make up for your parents' greed by giving donations to her ministry. Just visit her Website and you can easily fill out the necessary online forms to give her your money. (Just because God hooked her up with a few doctorates doesn't mean God is going to pay all the bills.)

9. Ibid., 208–9, 212. My comments on the reason for Jesus' death are, of course, satirical. The point is, the gospel of health and wealth assumed in her comments is at extremem odds with the life and teaching of Jesus—not to mention the prophets.

10. Ibid., 212.

She also claims that "the propensity to premenstrual syndrome (PMS) and difficult female cycles" can be related to a "curse of idolatry in the bloodline" which leads many women to the "curse of insanity."[11]

Is that why you ladies are so crazy once a month?[12]

Most intriguing of all, and my personal favorite, is her understanding of how it is possible that godly religious leaders could ever commit adultery. Given the rampant phenomenon of marital infidelity, especially in prominent religious and morally conservative politicians, there must be an answer explaining why they are just as likely to fall prey to this sinful behavior as many of their own heathen constituents. Well, there is an answer, claims Jacobs:

> One day I was praying for a top religious leader who seemingly had lost his senses, left his wife of many years for a younger woman and had absolutely no remorse. It is possible that witchcraft had been worked against him. I know of situations in which witches infiltrated the homes of Christian leaders and worked spells on the men of the family to get them to fall into adultery.[13]

Would that be Love Potion #9?

So, what Jacobs is telling us is that when married men, especially those pious important religious leaders she is so fond of, put their bodies into the bodies of women who are not their spouses, it is ultimately the fault of other women.

Awesome.

I cannot wait to use that one.

It's Adam an Eve all over again. It just makes me want to scream, "Damn you women! You just have to eat everything *and* force us to have sex with you, too, don't you?"

According to Jacobs, she should be greatly admired for delivering her prophetic message because it is very dangerous to expose the real reasons for things like poverty and an unusually heavy discharge. At one point she explains that while she was quoting material for use against witchcraft her

11. Ibid., 215.

12. To avoid any confusion, I am, obviously, being facetious. It's satire. Women are awesome. They represent only half of the insane people on this planet. On the off chance, however, that what Jacobs says is true, she should start a campaign that includes such slogans as, "Girls, you don't need Midol, you need Jesus!" Or, "Pamp(e)rin yourself with Jesus." Now, *that* would be a great bumper sticker.

13. Ibid., 42.

"computer screen started flickering and went gray" which resulted in her computer shutting down.[14] She said she immediately prayed to God that he would command her intercessors to pray harder as, obviously, they had grown lax.

I wonder what their prayer sounded like?

Maybe something like this: "Lord, I know there is much violence in this world. There is disease, starvation, death, sickness, poverty, war, hatred, SIDS, AIDS, diabetes, cancer, American Idol, and Barry Bonds, but please Lord, I only ask you this: Please don't let Sister Jacob's computer freeze again!"

Can you imagine having a group of intercessors praying for you every time your computer froze?

You could try buying a Mac.

Given a number of other theological claims she makes, I am hardly surprised she believes witches have the ability to freeze computers. One of my favorite claims of hers is that the Bible supposedly teaches that Jesus and his disciples were rich (primarily because they were Jews), and, therefore, Christians, upon following their Jewish lead, should be able to turn into gold everything we touch.

Racist stereotype aside, we got the Midas touch, baby.

I love how paganism is often resuscitated by its enemies.

Speaking of gold, apparently, and I did not know this, gold (specifically yellow gold) is "considered a Christian metal."[15] Really? By whom? Rich white people in the United States making a killing off the radically subversive teachings of a poor homeless Jew from Nazareth? I'm not entirely sure of her theological source. All I know is that, according to her, if you or someone you know starts wearing silver and is "refusing to wear gold jewelry" then you may have a Satanist on your hands.

Of course, I immediately invested in some cheap silver jewelry.

Anything for the cause.

Jacobs is certainly an entertaining read. While belittling people who believe in ghosts, she remains the epitome of all things rational as she claims that the occult is behind everything ranging from Pokemon to the draping of one's hair across the left eye to homosexuality. Can you imagine that? According to Jacobs, the Devil is not only behind the specific

14. Ibid., 20.
15. Ibid., 173.

haircuts of The Misfits, emo kids, and has-been skateboarders from the 80s (myself included), but the Devil is actually behind homosexuality.

Behind it.

Right there behind homosexuality.

One might even say, in the rear of it.

One last warning from Jacobs I should probably heed (but given the nature of my project I plan to do the opposite of) is this: If you happen to come across a Satanic altar, you know, just in your daily routine, or as she puts it, "as you are prayer walking," whatever you do, do not attempt to kick it over. Powerful curses, she claims, are often attached to such objects, and if you are not fully prepared, even your righteous attempt to vandalize some Satanic property can come back to bite you in the butt.[16]

Or, it could you turn you into a homosexual.

Maybe both, I don't know.

What I do know is that all this talk about homosexuality has me thinking about a few southern evangelical Christian universities, hair salons, and just what the two have taught me about Satan.

THE MASON TARWATERS OF THIS WORLD CONFRONT THE POLITICS OF PENIS FENCING

That's all a prophet is good for—
to admit somebody else is an ass or a whore.

—Flannery O'Connor (*The Violent Bear it Away*)

That guy was a homo . . .

—Pat Robertson

Despite being able to conduct a number of excellent interviews for this book, some of them never even had a chance. Many ministers were anxious to talk to me until they learned what it was I was seeking. Some initially responded positively to my emails or phone calls, only to distance themselves as quickly as possible once they got wind of what I was

16. Ibid., 167.

after. Some even cut me off before the interview started. One minister, an ex-Wesleyan-recently-turned-Baptist, employed in what used to be an Evangelical Lutheran Church that is now a non-denominational church, only lasted three questions. When I asked this "soul winner" (a self-referential title) about why he had been through so many different Protestant churches, he replied that he was simply looking for a place where people took the "word of God seriously, with no compromises." I recommended that perhaps he should try something other than Protestantism.

"How about the Anabaptists or even Catholicism?" I asked.

Given that he was armed with his online degree from Bob Jones University, I was pretty certain that neither Anabaptism nor Catholicism was a viable option. Turns out, he had never even heard of the Anabaptists—"What kind of Baptist did you say?" And the one thing he learned from Bob Jones University was that Catholicism was the enemy of all things Christian.

For my third question, I asked, "So, you're employed in what was an Evangelical Lutheran church, but has since become a non-denominational church. Why did they break away?"

"Over the issue of homosexuality," he responded.

Before I could push the question, he told me he had to call me back. Which he never did. Liar. But that's all right, because we actually had conversations about this before. When I lived in North Carolina we would occasionally get our hair cut by the same person who happened to be one of my favorite cousins (the pickings are rather slim). When my cousin wanted to mess with me, he would schedule us back to back. He knew it drove me crazy because I had to listen to this preacher go on and on about how everyone except him and his little clique were going to hell.

My cousin can be a real bastard sometimes.

On these very stressful days, I would have to endure incessant preaching about everything ranging from the age of the universe (6,000 years of course) to the correct way to baptize. You'll have to forgive me, I can't recall if it is immersion or sprinkling. All I know is that if you choose incorrectly, Jesus will vomit you out of his mouth and make sure you spend eternity gnashing your teeth.

"Outside of the one correct way to baptize, do you talk about anything of genuine importance?" I once asked. "Does anyone there actually care about the poor, the widowed, the orphans, the imprisoned, or is it just a contest over the most insignificant things you can think of?"

"We talk about very serious things, very political things," he told me. "And we do it all the time. Every Sunday from the pulpit we're talking about things that matter. We talk about the salvation of your soul and countless other things."

Given that many fundamentalist churches have adopted a thoroughly pagan account of the soul—an absolute unadulterated revival of Gnosticism—I informed him that his overwhelming concern with its salvation was hardly political. Indeed, his account of salvation perpetuates the depoliticized nature of both Christianity and the flesh. I could tell he wasn't listening to me. In typical self-authorizing fundamentalist mode, owing nothing to tradition, he had much to teach everyone else. Who knows? Maybe I would learn something.

I asked him to name something of importance they discuss in his church.

Something timely.

I was hoping for something in regards to war, poverty, the loss of adequate farmland, or perhaps, the terrorist training facility in Fort Benning, Georgia. Instead, this is what he gave me:

"We talk about how homosexuality is destroying this country."

Well, it is timely, I guess.

"Look what happened to Sodom and Gomorrah," he continued. "That's what's going to happen to us if we don't stand up against homosexuality."

I have to be honest, I really like the image of standing "up" against homosexuality.

It makes you think he was protesting a little too much.

Of course, it would not be the first time a conservative preacher found himself engaged in the very throes of his heated protest.

Poor Ted Haggard.

And Paul Barnes.

And Lonnie Latham, and John Paulk . . . and have you ever noticed that sometimes Christian evangelists seem to take Jesus too literally on his love for prostitutes?

"Actually, according to Ezekiel," I informed him, "the sin of Sodom and Gomorrah was not homosexuality, it was their inability to practice hospitality to the stranger. God says that they had an excess of food and ease, yet they did not care for the needy. It wasn't just a matter of certain sexual practices; they exercised the sin of gluttony, greed, and hoarding, as well as pride—all at the expense of the poor. So, God killed them. But that's just the inerrant Word of God, what do I know?"

(A hermeneutical moment of reflection: It seems that a faithful interpretation of this story requires that we rethink what it means to be a Sodomite. Sodomy, biblically speaking, could be argued to be the practice of having a savings account while other people starve. Now that would make an interesting "devotional" topic.)

Homosexuality is a hot topic for evangelical Christians. I've been informed by countless "authorities" on the subject, some of them even home-schooled, that global warming was invented by scientists in collusion with liberal universities in order to make us forget that the real problem with the world is homosexuality.

"If the world is heating up," a prominent Assembly of God minister in my hometown told me, "it's not because of carbon monoxide—"

"Actually," I interrupted, "I think its carbon dioxide that is the more—"

"Whatever. It's not because of that, but because of homosexuality. People better get used to it. It's going to get a whole lot hotter for those who do it and for those who tolerate it."

I think what disturbed me most about his commentary on global warming was how it was followed by what could only be described as a very jovial laugh. He was certainly happy about what he imagined to be the fate of homosexuals.

For any number of reasons, many of my conversations about the Devil would often come back to same-sex relations. When I would press ministers on this topic, many would claim that homosexuality stems from the influence of Satan since, as one Baptist minister informed me, "No reasonable person would ever engage in something so unnatural. It's simply unacceptable for humans to do such things."

"What do you mean unacceptable?" I asked. "You mean as a fact of life, or as—"

"As in it is unnatural," he stated, almost yelling. "God created Adam and Eve, not Adam and Steve."

Seriously? Do people really still say that?

Apparently so.

By the way, if God didn't create Steve, who did?

"Well, when you say unnatural," I asked him, "what exactly do you mean?"

"I don't know how to say it any simpler: homosexuality is not natural. Even dogs know that."

He chuckled at what he imagined to be his unassailable logic. I guess when you can invoke canine behavior for what it means to be human you may feel as if you have reached the apex of human thinking.

Then again, male dogs do lick and smell other male dogs' testicles.

It is, after all, quite natural to them.

By raising such questions, I am not trying to undermine the importance of sexual ethics for Christian discipleship. I am simply suggesting that appeals to something called nature, as a prescriptive guide to such discipleship, are likely to fail. There are, after all, incredibly unique sexual and reproductive practices within other species that certainly defy what some humans would consider to be natural. A few examples are, in order:

- shrimp, African reed frogs, and clownfish (among many other species) change sex (sorry Gloria Steinem, the clownfish has spoken)
- monkeys, birds, porcupines, and innumerable other creatures take pleasure in autoeroticism
- male seahorses give birth
- aphids are born pregnant (babies having babies, sheesh)
- dolphins, pigs, penguins, and many, many other creatures actually have sex for reasons other than procreation; some do it based on the need for social organization, while others do it simply because, it seems, they like it
- orangutans, squirrel monkeys, American bison, big horned sheep, giraffes, tamarins, black swans, mallards, lions, macaque, and countless other species display what humans would refer to as homosexual practices (some researchers claim that it is found in all species)
- male bottlenose dolphins have a terrible habit of cornering a female and taking turns with her while the female attempts to escape (bad Flipper, bad)
- female arachnids, amphipods, and various female insects are known for consuming their male mate after, and sometimes during, copulation

- male cane toads will try to have sex with other males—regardless if the male is dead or alive
- bonobos are considered to be a bisexual species where males and females will get it on with others of the same or different sex, with the vast majority of their sexual encounters being non-reproductive
- flatworms have both male and female organs, they engage in an activity called "penis fencing" in which two flatworms attempt to impregnate the other, the one who loses the duel becomes the female (sorry Luce Irigaray, the flatworm has spoken)

The above list is just a tiny example of sexual and reproductive practices that may or may not function as a sexual guide for humans. As I was going through this list, my rather high-strung Baptist friend was eying me suspiciously. He was thinking I was making this all up.

I then included one of my favorites, "Do you know what parthenogenesis is?" which I immediately realized was a stupid question.

"No," he responded.

"It's the ability of a creature to give birth without male insemination."

Silence.

Since he was still single, and had earlier confessed to holding out for marriage, he may have suddenly thought he had cause for concern.

I explained how female whipped-tail lizards reproduce. Two females get together and engage in some rather raunchy sexual behavior which many researchers suggest is a form of mimicry (one female imitates what a male would do if there were any males left). Through the act of females mimicking sex, the female lizard on the bottom of the act becomes pregnant. She gives birth, of course, to clones. They all have the exact same DNA. Komodo dragons can also reproduce through parthenogenesis. Certain species of bees and birds can do it, as well as some sharks. But who knows what other "unusual" and "aberrant" sexual and (non)reproductive behavior other creatures practice?

Such practices are, of course, for these creatures quite natural. We have an immensely tiny view of the world and the diversity of its various animal kingdoms. Before we start talking about what is natural and unnatural, and how we can use other species for making an argument about human behavior, we may want to spend a little bit of time studying the natural world. I always recommend beginning with the works of Jeffrey Masson, Jane Goodall, Marc Bekoff, and Franz De Waal.

After thinking about it for a few minutes, the young minister admitted that it may be the case that frogs and lizards have strange sexual practices (it's not strange to them) but because of "The Fall," we cannot look at nature for a guide for how we are to behave.

"Exactly," I said. "I understand that there is a difference, theologically speaking, between creation and post-lapsarian nature, yet that is just what you tried to do when you were talking about human sexuality."

He then proceeded to lecture me on how the fall was the work of the Devil, and how through the fall all of creation was perverted. "Males and females" he told me, "are supposed to be together, but due to the Devil's intervention, creation's sexual and reproductive practices no longer bear the original design."

"So," I asked, "without the fall, Darwinian frogs would not puke up their young and monkeys would not masturbate?"

"Not in a perfect world."

Says the human.

Perhaps we should ask the monkey.

After discussing a number of prejudices engrained in some of the students trained at Bob Jones University, I was asked what I thought of Liberty University. You see, living in North Carolina means that you are surrounded by a large number of ministers trained at either Bob Jones or Liberty University. Few people are indifferent to these schools. One either loves them or loathes them. Given that I tend to be concerned about things like equality, the environment, and the general well-being of all living things, I tend to fall into the loathing camp. So, when I was asked what I thought about Liberty, I answered, "Well, save for the rather racist, sexist, anti-Catholic, and generally xenophobic history of the school, it may not be all bad. Then again, it could be."

At that moment, the hairstylist (again, my cousin—who, suspiciously, was also the one who asked me the question about Liberty), turned to the person in his chair and asked the lady whose hair he was cutting, "Your husband is a minister isn't he? Where did he go to school?"

The woman turned in her chair, eyed me coolly, and said, "Liberty University."

Oops.

I'm not going to lie. I laughed out loud. Seriously, I did. I genuinely laughed out loud. Many people would be embarrassed by a situation such as that, and, maybe, deep down I too was embarrassed and my laughter was simply a result of such embarrassment.

Then again, I think I found it really funny.

I've always wondered if my cousin did that to me on purpose.

Points for him.

After laughing for a few seconds, I noticed she was still staring at me. Since she refused to alter her stare, and guessing she already thought me a major asshole, I decided to confirm her suspicions.

"Well," I ventured, "do you have anybody who goes to your church, or for that matter, anybody who you consider to be your friend that is gay, black, or Catholic? Or, for that matter, how about Hispanic? There are lots of Hispanics in this area, and what do you know, most of them are Catholic. That would be a double whammy, huh?"

Still looking like she was about to come out of her chair and beat the "tar" out of me (as we Southerners are found of saying), she said, "I'll have you know I have lots of friends who are black."

"Do they know this?"

At this point, she became visibly angry and started swinging around in her chair. It was all so amusing as my cousin kept on cutting. The whole time he had this ridiculous grin on his face as if he were enjoying himself. It was either that or he had just taken a chunk out of her hair. Either way, he was having a good time.

She threw a few harsh words at me; I can't recall the specifics. I do remember thinking we were in a pretty small salon and this left me wondering if a Mennonite could take a Baptist.

Probably neither in theory nor reality.

When she left, there was this other woman cheerfully watching the whole fiasco. She stood up and said, "I just can't stand a racist."

As she waited her turn to get her hair cut, she started talking about her daughter's upcoming marriage. She told us all about the plans for the wedding, the wedding dress, the rehearsal dinner, the reception, the cake, the church, the flowers, the musicians, the wedding director, her future son-in-law, all of her future in-laws for that matter, and pretty much everything else I have ever found to be sleep-inducing.

Nevertheless, I asked her if she liked her future son-in-law. She replied that he was "nice enough" and "held down" a good job. "They'll make beautiful babies," she told me.

"Well, if your daughter looks anything like you," I said with a grin, "then her children will have to be beautiful."

You can take the boy out of the South, but you cannot take the South of the boy.

"You are a charmer, aren't you?" she asked.

"I don't think Miss Liberty would agree."

She nodded her head, and then proceeded to tell me the exact reasons why her children would be so beautiful. Apparently, her daughter was very fair-skinned with a light complexion. Her husband, on the other hand, had a very dark complexion.

"When I first met him, I thought maybe he was from Mexico or something. Or, that maybe his parents were Mexican. But, no, they are all full-bloodied Americans."

I informed her that Mexicans are American, too.

"America is not just the United States," I told her. "We're simply part of what is referred to as the Americas."

She seemed baffled by the geographical lesson, but not quite baffled enough to prohibit her from clarifying her position.

"Well, you know what I mean. *American* Americans."

I confessed to being unfamiliar with such terminology. I'm going to go out on a limb and assume Ann Coulter or Rush Limbaugh concocted that one.

I asked her if it would have mattered if he did happen to be Mexican, if she would have protested their marriage.

"Well, now listen. I don't like this any more than you do, but the truth is . . . I would have a problem with their marriage. What concerned parent wouldn't be bothered by it? This is not because I'm racist you understand, but because our culture is racist. It's just not fair to the children they would create. They would just get made fun of for being *mixed*. I just think its best if people stay in their own race."

"I'm sure you do," I responded. "But, hey, at least *you're* not racist."

It's interesting to reflect back on these stories as I continue my search for Satan. Many of these ministers, and spouses of ministers, left thinking I was a pompous jerk. Maybe I was a pompous jerk, but I would like to think I was being a pompous jerk for the right reasons. The geographical culture that raised me, a culture that in many ways I deeply love, has historically harbored much hostility for people who are gay, or are of a different race, nationality, or faith tradition (even within Christianity). The fact that this same culture shares a fascination with the Devil is not, I think, a coincidence. Indeed, I think the southern Protestant's love affair with the diabolical one is so rich that not even Flannery O'Connor could perfectly record it.

I mention O'Connor because she was such a phenomenal writer who took seriously the religiosity of the South, its characters, and the reality of the Devil. Her work is mired in both the beauty and ugliness constitutive of the landscape and characters of the South. She was enamored by the southern Protestant's ability to take seriously both God and the Devil. This often resulted in the creation of characters who sometimes seem rather comical, bizarre, and, occasionally, downright monstrous. It also resulted in the creation of some unbelievably accurate and honest portrayals of devout Christians attempting to navigate the dangerous terrain known as "the world." Such a navigation required that O'Connor create characters who understood all of life through the lens that is the Bible. For these characters, there is a divine drama being played out for the possession of their very embodied souls. The Devil is waging war with God for the possession of God's creation. Though God has already won the war (through the incarnation, death, and resurrection of Jesus), the Devil can still cause a whole hell of a lot of trouble for those of us still caught in the time between times. For O'Connor, the problem was not with taking God, the Bible, or the Devil seriously, it was when God was used to create or perpetuate comfortable illusions about our very grasp on God. She once described her project as "the action of grace in a territory held largely by the devil."[17] She desired to penetrate, probe, and break down the illusions we have created about ourselves by crafting powerful characters who, while both comic and tragic, are there to shock us into understanding that "every word they utter is true." The Devil was a genuine reality for O'Connor. She claimed that "our salvation is played out with the Devil . . . a Devil who is not simply generalized evil, but an evil intelligence determined by its own supremacy. . . I want to be certain that the Devil gets identified as the Devil and not simply taken for this or that psychological tendency."[18]

17. This is quoted in Russell, *Prince of Darkness*, 267.
18. Ibid., 268.

If O'Connor is correct, that is, if the Devil is real, then I have no doubt that I experienced his power in some of these beauty salon conversations. It is, sometimes, too difficult for me to fathom how so many people, especially Christians, could figure out how to be so xenophobic without a little bit of help.

Despite my lack of optimism in human nature, I continually remain surprised by the ease in which so many God-fearing people, of all stripes, demonize the other. I'm learning much about Satan, but it's not what I expected to learn. I'm learning that Satan keeps a coterie of company that includes Darwinians, Hindus, Muslims, Catholics, homosexuals, pagans, bonobos, penguins, Wiccans, and, apparently, Nigerians. Absolutely across the board, with what has literally been countless interviews and conversations, almost every discussion about Satan has resulted in the person who believes in Satan ascribing to a group other than their own a Satanic status. To be fair, I'm going to include encounters with representatives of some of those groups in the latter two chapters (I tried to interview some bonobos, but they were more interested in food and sex than demons and the apocalypse). If these demonized groups are truly satanic, then perhaps I have been looking in all the wrong places. It may be time to step up the search.

3 RUNNING WITH THE DEVIL

Christianity has a built-in defense system: anything that questions a belief, no matter how logical the argument is, is the work of Satan by the very fact that it makes you question a belief. It's a very interesting defense mechanism and the only way to get by it—and believe me, I was raised Southern Baptist—is to take massive amounts of mushrooms, sit in a field, and just go, "Show me."

—Bill Hicks

While chapters 4 and 5 are going to include a number of groups that may hold the key to Satan's location, I will first examine a small number of biblical passages that deal specifically with either Satan or his demons. To be sure, there are numerous passages that, due to constraints on space, I cannot address in this chapter, but I hope to at least continue to note some of them throughout the remainder of the book. The particular passages I am including in this chapter seem to hold many possibilities for how we have come to understand God and God's pseudo-rival. Perhaps by taking a closer look at a few of these passages we can make some sense out of the claims in chapters 1 and 2, as well as those to come in chapters 4 and 5. By looking closely at a few of these passages, I hope to be able to gain a better sense of where some of our culture's thinking about Satan originates. Hopefully this will shed some light, or darkness, on the best course for how to proceed in my search.

NEVER BET AGAINST THE HOUSE

Then I was right. Job has all his children killed, and Michael Bay gets to keep making movies. There isn't a God.

—Kyle Broflovski (Trey Parker and Matt Stone, *Southpark*)

"Damn," interrupted one of my female students. "Can you imagine how wrecked her vagina must be?"

I'll admit to being a bit taken back by her question. After recovering from my feeble attempt to hide my now strawberry-colored face I responded with, "I, uh, well, I never really thought about it."

"Of course you didn't," she replied. "You're a man."

This is true. I was born with the XY chromosome.

The vagina in question my student was referring to belonged to Job's wife. We were discussing the issue of theodicy and were spending a few days talking about the Book of Job. It is a lovely book. It's one of those books that actually raises more questions than answers. At its best, the Book of Job completely deconstructs all of our questions in regards to the goodness of God in light of so much evil and suffering, while at its worst, it completely deconstructs all of our questions in regards to the goodness of God in light of so much evil and suffering.

Which is exactly why I like it.

I'm guessing that when the ecclesial officials decided to include the Book of Job in its canon someone was thinking, "Well, this should keep Christians perplexed for a few thousand years."

Job well done.

My student's concern for Job's wife occurred at the end of the book where we find Job being "blessed" with ten brand new kids.

"That's not much of a blessing for the wife," my student protested. "Plus," she continued, "can you imagine how much pain she had to endure? I mean, there were no epidurals then!"

"Yeah," chimed in one of my male students. "But I bet by the time she got to number sixteen they were just falling out."

I do love teaching college students.

"But that's not even the point," stated my young female scholar. "I was being a bit rhetorical anyway. I'm just offended that the author of this book thought it was a positive thing to include this part about Job getting brand new kids to replace the others. Is this our reward for being submissive? That after God allowed Satan, or even dared Satan for that matter, to kill all of their kids, God would just reward them with ten more as if to say, 'Look, it's all better. You didn't really like those other ten anyway. Now get on your knees and thank me.' Are we supposed to take that as a good thing? Who thought it was a good idea to include this book in the Bible?"

Now those are the kinds of questions a theology professor enjoys receiving.

As just stated, the Book of Job does raise a number of important questions. Despite completely leveling the idea that God rewards virtue and punishes vice, God still gives everything back to Job at the end of the story. I often wonder if this does not, in some very real way, contradict the gist of the book. Then again, it definitely reinforces the notion that the rain certainly falls on the just and unjust alike. To put it crudely, I sometimes think that what the Book of Job is ultimately saying is, "I don't care how faithful you are to God, you can still get seriously screwed in this life."

The trick is discovering who is responsible for the screwing. Actually, I think that's kind of the heart of theodicy. Who's holding the Phillips-head?

Theodicy is the attempt to justify the ways of God to God's creation. Though this may strike some as being inherently problematic or entirely presumptuous, we should be reminded that many of the Psalms, the Book of Lamentations, and even Jesus on the cross, raised a few important questions about the fidelity of God. It's not a bad thing that God's creation is concerned with issues of justice. According to God, we're supposed to be concerned with issues of justice. Though we may never be able to comprehend the ways of God, the fact that we are driven to understand what may appear to be meaningless suffering in this world—in light of Christianity's claim that God is omniscient, loving, and beneficent—simply means that we have been instilled with an affinity for goodness.

This is a good thing.

It's also a dangerous thing.

It's dangerous because we may end up with questions, and answers, that no longer sit well with us. Such questions and answers may no longer comfort us. This too is not a bad thing. If nothing else, we can prove Feuerbach and Marx wrong by having the kind of faith that is not always, if ever, comfortable.

What my student and the rest of us were discussing was how to square the prominent claim that God is good, loving, and all-powerful with the existence of evil. In this regard, the Book of Job is a wonderful place to begin (and/or end).

We began with the first chapter of the Book of Job. Included below is the first section I always read to my students along with a few scattered questions I have for the text. I'm citing from the New Revised Standard Version (with apologies to Brother Ray for not using his preferred seventeenth-century King James translation):

> One day the heavenly beings came to present themselves before the Lord and Satan also came among them. The Lord said to Satan, "Where have you come from? [*I have often wondered if this was a rhetorical question. Did God really not know where Satan had been?*] "From going to and fro on the earth and walking up and down on it." The Lord said to Satan, "Have you considered my servant Job? There is no one like him on the earth, a blameless and upright man who fears God and turns away from evil." [*Okay, so it must have been rhetorical as God and Satan clearly had a conversation about this subject prior to Satan's roaming up and down on the earth.*] Then Satan answered the Lord, "Does Job fear God for nothing? Have you not put a fence around him and his house and all that he has, on every side? You have blessed the work of his hands, and his possessions have increased in the land. [*So, does God reward good behavior?*] But stretch out your hand now, and touch all that he has, and he will curse you to your face." The Lord said to Satan, "Very well, all that he has is in your power; only do not stretch out your hand against him!" So Satan went out from the presence of the Lord. (1:6–12)

The next seven verses detail the loss of Job's livestock, most of his servants (save for four of them—someone has to be left alive to bring the bad news), and all of Job's children. The blame was dropped on the Sabeans, Chaldeans, a great wind, and, interestingly enough, God (1:16). Little, if no time at all, was wasted on Job's undoing.

Job reacted the way most people would react in such a situation: he tore his clothes, shaved his head, and immediately worshipped God. Well, perhaps his behavior was slightly different than the average Joe's, or Job's (sorry). Dismayed by it all, Satan returns to heaven (by chapter 2) only to face the exact same conversation as found in chapter 1. Though there is one slight difference: God asks Satan if he has considered Job, the most blameless and upright person on earth, only to add, "He still persists in his integrity, although you incited me against him, to destroy him for no reason." What a remarkable thing for God to confess to Satan. God was *incited* against Job to destroy him for *no reason*. If it was really for "no reason," then why do it? Already by the second chapter my students and I are getting the strange idea that this is just a game, or even worse, a wager in which no one can possibly be a winner. Nevertheless, despite already being incited by Satan once for no reason, God concedes and does it again—and presumably for, again, no reason.

Job 2:4–6 states: "Then Satan answered the Lord, 'Skin for skin! All that people have they will give to save their lives. But stretch out your hand now and touch his bone and his flesh, and he will curse you to your face.' The Lord said to Satan, 'Very well, he is in your power; only spare his life.'"

A few of my closer readers will note that Satan suggests it is God who will stretch out God's hand in order to bring physical pain on Job, despite God immediately placing such power in the hands of Satan. Though God forbids the killing of Job, as that would be rather reckless since there can be no clear winner of this divine wager if the one being bet upon is dead, God does grant Satan the power to harm Job. This, of course, quickly raises the question of who is really responsible for the forthcoming physical ailments that Job is going to suffer for thirty some chapters: God or Satan?

Most of us know the rest of the story. Job is afflicted with all sorts of sores, his wife tells him to curse God and die, a number of "comforters" come to tell him that he obviously did something wrong and, presumably deserves it, and yet, through it all, Job remains steadfast and loyal to God. For the vast majority of this book Job does nothing but suffer the loss of his family, his servants, his livestock, his livelihood, bodily comforts, and, what I imagine to be worst of all, he had to endure the incessant theologizing of his best friends. Indeed, if I have learned anything from the Book of Job it is that when you are with someone suffering immense pain and suffering, just shut up and be there for them. Don't try to make yourself feel better by attempting to explain it away.

Though Job is sticking the course, he still cannot help but wonder why he is suffering what seems to be intentionally designed calamities (as we, the readers, know he has been intentionally targeted). For thirty plus chapters, Job's endurance of suffering, along with his bafflement as to why he is suffering, finally provokes a response out of God. Why is Job undergoing so much physical and emotional pain? Why did he have to lose his very own children who were merely innocent bystanders in the midst of this bet? What did the sheep, oxen, donkeys, and all the humans killed in this wager between God and Satan ever do to deserve their deaths? Never fear, God spends four chapters addressing these concerns:

> Then the Lord answered Job out of the whirlwind: "Who is this that darkens counsel by words without knowledge? Gird up your loins like a man, I will question you, and you shall declare to me. [*Uh-oh.*] Where were you when I laid the foundation of the earth? Tell me if you have any understanding. Who determined its measurements—surely you must know. [*And I thought I had a penchant for being sassy.*] . . . Have you commanded the morning since your days began, and cause the dawn to know its place . . . have you entered in the springs of the sea, or walked in the recesses of the deep? Have the gates of death been revealed to you, or have you seen the gates of deep darkness? Have you comprehended the expanse of the earth? Declare, if you know all this. (Job 38:1–5, 12, 16–18)

"Okay, okay, I get it, I get it," says Job. "You're great, wonderful, all knowing, all powerful, you know when the mountain goat feeds its young, yada, yada, yada—but could you just explain why you subjected me to so much pain and misery? Could you just tell me *why* you killed my children?"

God's response?

"To win a bet."

All right, so, I made that part up. Call it reading between the lines. I like to delve into the text.

Rather, for three consecutive chapters God reminds Job how majestic God is (given Job's righteousness it seems highly unlikely that he had forgotten), and that if anyone is going to be asking questions, it will be God. In the last chapter, Job states his regret for even attempting to understand what was going on. Job says, "I despise myself, and repent in dust and ashes" (Job 42:6).

To be clear, this book does conclude with a fairy tale ending. Job and his unnamed wife receive ten more children, brand new livestock, and an even better set up than previously. (Come on Disney, it's your next big animated hit!) Still, I really wish I could ask Job about it. I just want to ask him one question. Despite the fact that I think I already know the answer, I still want to ask him, "Job, was it worth it?"

I think it's an honest question. Would you be good with your children dying in order for God to prove Satan wrong?

Of course, that's where it gets tricky. Does God really *need* to prove to Satan Job's righteousness? If not, then why do it? Plus, if Satan is aware of God's omniscience, and I am guessing Satan is, then why would Satan be foolish enough to make a bet that he knows he cannot win? You never bet against the house—especially when the house has foreknowledge of future events! Yet, this makes it even more scandalous. After all, the only real loser in this story is Job—or, actually, Job's deceased children, servants, and livestock. Satan didn't lose anything. As a matter of fact, if Satan is as cunning as the Bible suggests, and if he is only playing the role that God has assigned him, that of the adversary, then Satan was aware of what he was doing the whole time. Satan knew what would happen, just like God already knew what would happen. Yet, despite God's foreknowledge God acts against Job anyway. It was God who claimed that Satan incited God against Job—twice. So who was really playing whom in this divine wager, and to what end? Didn't Satan win just as much as God? I just cannot make sense as to why Satan comes out as the bad guy in this story. Everything that happens to Job occurs only because God grants Satan special permission to torment Job. It would be like my older, larger brother asking our dad if he can beat me up and our dad saying, "Sure, beat him up, burn his stuff, destroy his livelihood, just don't kill him." Who should I be mad at? To ascribe guilt to Satan would be to suggest that Satan really does have power over God, as it would assume that Satan can incite God against God's own creation (or, to extend my poor analogy, that my brother could force our father's hand). Satan may or may not be deified in this story, depending on how you read it, yet we would be wise to not cast blame on Satan for what occurs to Job. After all, it was God who first chose Job for the wager. It was God who on two separate occasions permitted the havoc wrought on Job. Finally, it was God who blasted Job for even thinking about why he should be so unfortunate as to suffer such a horrific array of events. So, how does this story, one that I am incredibly fond of, help me in my search for the Evil One?

I have no idea.

One of my students, rather unintentionally, helped me make a little sense of this Jobian quandary. Granted, I don't think it's going to make me sleep any better at night, but it is worth considering. He said, "You know, it's a scary thing to be one of God's favorites. Not just for you, but, as we learned from this story, for your loved ones. It makes you a little nervous if your parents are righteous people."

It is true; the closer you are to God the more likely you are to experience a world of hurt. If you don't believe me, first, stop listening to Joel Osteen, and, second, just ask Job, Abraham, Moses, Jeremiah, Isaiah, Jonah, Hosea, the disciples, the martyrs, the majority of saints throughout Christian history, pretty much the entire history of the Jewish people and . . . it seems like I am forgetting someone . . . oh yeah, Jesus.

"My God, my God, why have you forsaken me?"

Because your Father loves you—and us—so much.

It *is* one hell of a story.

THE FIRST ETHICIST DISCUSSES THE IMPOSSIBILITY OF HIS FALL

This serpent, Satan, is not the enemy of Man, but He who made Gods of our race, knowing Good and Evil.

—Aleister Crowley

Only against God can man know good and evil.

—Dietrich Bonhoeffer

Assuming that Satan is the ruler of the air or the god of this world (2 Cor 4:4), and that Satan is possessing the minds and bodies of countless millions in order to lead them away from God—the very God that created this once-good being—we must ask the question: How did Satan fall from his perfectly created state of being?

This is a question that tends to follow conversations revolving around the aforementioned problem of theodicy. For instance, many of my students will quickly pass over the trouble of pain and suffering in this world with the inevitable response of free will. My students tell me it is the freedom God grants us to make our own decisions that explains the presence of pain and suffering.

"Then what's so great about free will?" I'll often ask. "Let's get rid of it and enjoy paradise."

"But we have to have free will," my students protest. "Otherwise our decision to serve God will not be a legitimate decision."

Playing the devil's advocate, I push forward: "Well, better an illegitimate decision, or a lack of a decision altogether, if that means no more cancer, war, hunger, earthquakes, tornadoes, tsunamis, and steroids in baseball. It seems to me like this whole free will thing is a bit overrated. Plus, how does it explain the decision to disobey God *prior* to the fall?"

Such a question normally elicits blank stares.

"But we have the choice to disobey God," a student meekly offers.

"Right, but how do you explain the ability to disobey God *prior* to the fall? I understand how free will addresses the problems concerned with theodicy *after* the fall, just not before it."

More blank stares.

"Okay," I tell them, "let's start at the beginning."

At this point we delve into the standard fare that follows from the free will argument. In the beginning God created everything and it was good. After creating the stars, various universes, bodies of water, nonhuman animals, the angelic court, etc., God creates an animal that is in God's image: humans. These humans, along with everything else, are good. Why are they good? Because God created them. Simple enough.

Life is pretty fantastic for the first humans, that being Adam and Eve, as they enjoy the paradisal Garden of Eden. They have everything they could ever want: food, sex, and immediate communion with God. God, however, does place one limitation on Adam and Eve: God tells them not to eat of the tree of knowledge; otherwise they will die. At this point, someone usually queries as to why God put the tree of knowledge there in the first place, and this is where we normally encounter the notion of free will.

"God puts the tree there in order to provide the option as to whether or not to obey God," a student argues.

Of course, this makes God out to be a lot more like Satan than some of us are comfortable with as, traditionally speaking, Satan is the tempter, not God. Nevertheless, for free will to exist there has to be some kind of choice between obeying God and disobeying God, therefore the tree of knowledge becomes a providentially ordered logical necessity.

This does not, however, address how it is possible for Adam and Eve actually to disobey God. The option is not enough of an explanation. "How was it possible," I ask my students, "for humans, who were created good, and therefore should only be able to will the good, choose to do the opposite of good? There should be no real choice in the matter. Regardless of how you take the story of Adam and Eve, literally or not, this should not have been a real choice because they should not be able to decide to disobey God. This would suggest a flaw in their pre-lapsarian nature, but as we know, they were created good, and, therefore, at least at this point, should only be able to will the good. For them to do anything other than this would require that a good creation will to do evil, which they cannot because they only know the good. So, how is it possible that Adam and Eve disobeyed God?"

"Easy," claims a student sounding like Napoleon Dynamite. "Satan influenced them to do it. It's in Genesis chapter 3."

Despite our inability to locate Satan in Genesis chapter 3, we did conclude that since the majority of the Christian tradition assumes that the serpent in the Garden of Eden is a manifestation of Satan, we would permit a rather anachronistic reading into the text.

"Satan made them do it," claims the same student, "or at least tempted them to do it."

"Well," I suggest, "let us examine the text."

> Now the serpent was more crafty than any other wild animal that the Lord God had made. [*Note that, being "crafty" is not necessarily bad. The word can mean "sly" but it can also mean "prudent" as it is used in Proverbs 12:16. Plus, as noted, it is the "Lord God" who made the serpent, who, at this point, is still a perfectly good creature living in a perfectly good garden.*] He said to the woman, "Did God say, 'You shall not eat from any tree in the garden?'" The woman said to the serpent, "We may eat of the fruit of the trees in the garden; but God said, 'You shall not eat of the fruit of the tree that is in the middle of the garden, nor shall you touch it, or you shall die.'" But the serpent said to the woman, "You will not die; for God knows that when you eat of it your eyes will be opened, and you will be like God, knowing good and evil." So when the woman saw that the tree was good for food, and that it was a delight to the eyes, and that the tree was to be desired to make one wise, she took of its fruit and ate; and she also gave some to her husband, who was with her, and he ate. Then the eyes of both were opened, and they

knew that they were naked; and they sewed fig leaves together and
made loincloths for themselves. (Gen 3:1–7)

The passage continues with God looking for Adam and Eve in the
garden, while they hide due to their shame of being nude. God asked
them how they knew they were naked (God is quite the rhetorician), and
upon finding out that they had partaken of the forbidden fruit, immediately stripped the serpent of its legs (I'm guessing it originally looked like
a Komodo dragon), increased birth pangs in women (which is why epidurals are thoroughly eschatological), and increased the labor required
to grow food (making it necessary to pay close attention to people like
Wendell Berry).

The story is an interesting one if for no other reason than the half-
truth told by the serpent. The serpent lied in claiming that they would not
die, but he spoke the truth when he said that God did not want them to
eat of the tree, for it would make them like God.

They would, that is, know the difference between good and evil.

God does not deny this; rather, God affirms the serpent's claim: "Then
the Lord God said, 'See, the man has become like one of us, knowing
good and evil'" (Gen 3:22). Realizing that Adam and Eve would now eat
of the tree of life, therein becoming immortal, God banishes them from
the garden. Despite Christianity's hope for eternal life, partaking of the
tree of life, at least at this point, seems to be a bad thing. (And what was
the tree doing there in the first place?) What is definitely a bad thing is the
knowledge of good and evil. One of the most prominent theologians of
the twentieth century, Dietrich Bonhoeffer, argued that the pursuit of ethics is little more than the perpetuation of original sin. Ethics is the attempt
to know good and evil without knowing God, and, therefore, should not
be practiced. Christians, if they are to be Christian, must be amoralists.[1]

This is, hopefully, a rather scandalous claim. Christians (and Jews
and Muslims for that matter) should not practice ethics if ethics means
knowing the difference between good and evil without knowing God.
That's called atheism. This does not mean that atheists are satanic—
though most of the people included in the first two chapters would think
so. What it means is, ethicists are satanic.

I should probably rethink where I conduct my research.

---

1. Cf. Bonhoeffer, *Ethics*, 17–20; and Milbank, *Word Made Strange*, 219–32.

The main problem I have with such a claim is that the majority of "professional" ethicists I know are just alcoholics who drive hybrids. They don't appear to be anymore satanic than the non-ethicist. I guess Hannah Arendt was right: evil really is banal.

Of course, the idea here is that any reliance upon a system of differentiating good from evil that is somehow absent the knowledge of God is the great serpentine temptation. One need not be a professional or a paid ethicist to do this, one need only be concerned with the good separate from God.

Like I said, alcoholics driving hybrids.

To get back to the task at hand, this story is still not terribly helpful in terms of finding out how evil found its way in creation. Even if we concede that the serpent tempted humans to disobey God, therein creating the fall, it still does not explain how the serpent fell prior to the fall.

"Well, the serpent is Satan," claims one of my students as if that somehow resolves the issue.

"Fair enough," I respond. "But who is Satan?"

"A fallen angel," replies my student.

"And just how did Satan fall?" I inquire.

"Pretty hard," claims another student attempting to be clever.

"Well, this may be true, and if Dante is correct, pretty far, too. But how," I ask my students, "was it possible for Satan to fall?"

I explain to them that, according to Christian orthodoxy, Satan is a creation of God. Since everything God created was created good, Satan was a good creation. For Satan to fall there must have first been an option for choosing to disobey God, indicating that evil was optional prior to Satan choosing it. Yet, this would assume there is evil to choose prior to the choosing of it. Is such a thing possible in a creation yet to be marred by disobedience? Also, as with Adam and Eve, how is it possible for Satan to fall if Satan is created good? Satan should only be able to will the good. Satan could not, originally, fall from his own volition because his own non-fallen volition could only will the good. Before I allow my students to answer with free will, I explain how free will only makes sense after the fall. Free will, to paraphrase John Milbank, is a fiction created as a result of the fall.[2] It is the story created to make sense of disobeying God once our nature is no longer good, but it cannot make sense of how, when our nature was

2. Milbank, *Being Reconciled*, 8.

good and we could only will the good, we could somehow choose the non-good. It is understandable how we are capable of choosing to disobey God now that we reside in a post-lapsarian world, for we are, as Scripture says, "wicked from birth." But how was it possible for us to fall prior to the fall, when, at that point, we could only rightly desire not to fall? To risk using the word "fall" one too many times, we can only fall after the fall.

Again, my concerns are normally met with glossed-over faces. Once a student even threw something at me. Fortunately, her aim was not particularly good.

This is not simply a mind game or a wicked bit of fun I have with my students; this is a very serious theological issue. Even Augustine, the church's most influential theologian, admitted that on this particular point we must pass with darkness and silence: "The truth is that one should not try to find an efficient cause for a wrong choice. It is not a matter of efficiency but of deficiency; the evil will itself is not effective but defective. . . . To try to discover the causes of such defection—deficient, not efficient cause—is like trying to see darkness or to hear silence."[3]

We cannot, of course, see darkness nor hear silence, but we are aware of them through the absence of perception. Augustine is claiming that since God creates *ex nihilo*, out of nothing, evil cannot exist. It has no tangible reality. We cannot claim evil exists for it has no substance. Whatever evil is, if it *is* anything, is simply a lack of good (*privatio boni*). Therefore, looking for an effective cause that led to the fall is akin to attempting to see darkness. It cannot be done. To make the matter slightly more confusing Augustine states, "No one therefore must try to get to know from me what I know that I do not know, unless, it may be, in order to learn not to know what must be known to be incapable of being known!"[4]

Thank you St. Augustine. I can proceed with my intellectually confusing antics only because you were the master of it.

What is at stake in this conversation is not only the question of theodicy (a particularly modern, and rather tiresome, question from an orthodox Christian perspective), but the more intriguing question of the role and fall of Satan. In the Old Testament, Satan is an angel of God doing the Lord's bidding. He is the adversary, the accuser of humanity, who is merely doing that which God created him to do. Satan is simply the created instru-

---

3. Augustine *City of God* 12.7 (Battenson, 479–80). .
4. Ibid. (480).

ment of God who, like any other angel, does what he is commanded to do. Sometimes it is confusing to determine which actions belong to God and which belong to Satan, as in the case when David took a census of his people. Second Samuel 24:1 claims, "[T]he anger of the Lord was kindled against Israel, and he incited David against them, saying, 'Go, count the people of Israel and Judah.'" First Chronicles 21:1, on the other hand, claims that it was "Satan" who "stood up against Israel, and incited David to count the people of Israel."[5] Whoever or whatever Satan is in the Old Testament, he is not the diabolical Devil found in the New Testament. How Satan fell, or even when Satan fell (thus, in a sense, becoming the Devil), has been subject to debate for about two thousand years. At this point, I don't really care how or when Satan fell, I just want to find him without having to travel through either the nine levels of hell or yet another ethics conference. Perhaps a few New Testament texts will prove enlightening.

TURNING WATER INTO WINE AND DEMONS INTO SWINE

Thou shall not kill. Thou shall not commit adultery. Do not eat pork.

I'm sorry, what was that last one?

Don't eat pork. God has spoken.

Is that the word of God or is that pigs trying to outsmart everybody?

—Jon Stewart

Maybe it began with *The Lord of the Flies*, but I'm going to go out on a limb and suggest that the association of pigs with evil stems from a slightly older tradition. Christopher Hitchens, a journalist/literary critic who on most occasions I would be embarrassed to quote, argues that "the cloven hoof, or trotter, became a sign of diabolism to the fearful, and I daresay that it is easy to surmise which came first—the devil or the pig."[6]

5. There is also the case of 1 Kgs 22:19–23 where it is not Satan who receives blame for lying prophets, but God: "So you see, the Lord has put a lying spirit in the mouth of all these your prophets; the Lord has decreed disaster for you."

6. Hitchens, *God is not Great*, 38.

Granted, Christian orthodoxy claims that all of creation is good, every living creature ranging from howler monkeys to basilisks are manifestations of God's infinite wisdom. Unfortunately, however, lions kill gazelles, humans poach rhinos, and jellyfish attack surfers. Perhaps I should not say attack, but when that jellyfish wrapped its tentacles around my leg and nailed me with its cnidocytes I was vehemently cursing God's lovely creation. I was cursing just loud enough to attract the attention of a number of beach-goers, and as I made my way back to the shore I was greeted by a ten-year-old offering me a cup of some sort of unnamed liquid meant to neutralize the sting.

"Is that vinegar?" I asked.

"Nope," said the kid.

He just continued staring at me, oblivious to the fact that I was still waiting to hear what was in the cup.

"Well," I asked, "what is it?"

"Don't ask so many questions; just pour it on your leg."

"No thanks," I told him.

"Whatever," replied the kid. "I was actually stung by one yesterday."

"What did you do? Pour this 'stuff' on it?"

"Nah, I just played it off. It's not like I'm a *baby* or anything."

Well, I am a baby. I neither poured the mysterious liquid on my leg, nor did I play it off. I was done for the day. The jellyfish were everywhere. But it did make me think about the ongoing goodness of God's creation in light of the fall. It reminded me that whatever the peaceable kingdom is going to look like, it will not contain jellyfish stinging surfers. Granted, if that's the worst thing that ever happens to a surfer, we're in pretty good shape. I don't even like to think about the large variety of sharks hunting in shallow waters.

Back to pigs.

Despite Christianity's claim that all creation is good, and fallen creation will be redeemed, pigs have had it rough. By this I am not simply referring to factory farming that systematically slaughters millions of pigs a year in order to produce cheap food resulting in the poor health of humans. If all Jews, Christians, and Muslims actually kept the dietary commands found in their shared Hebrew Bible, we would at least be saving the lives of countless pigs. (Though the holocaust of propitiary turtledoves would have long since laid waste to countless ecosystems.) Of course, it is that very same Bible that has created some unique thinking in regards to swine. The dietary laws forbid God's chosen people to consume, along with various other animals, pigs. Many modern scholars suggest that the reason pigs were considered unclean is that if they were not cooked properly one could contract the worms of trichinosis. The story goes, speculates the modern apologete, that the ancient Israelites forbade the consumption of swine due to the large number of people who became sick and died after eating.

Though it is the case that pigs, if you are going to eat them, should be cooked properly, this interpretation is simply absent from the text. Deuteronomy gives a very clean-cut interpretation as to why God's chosen people must consider pigs unclean: they divide the hoof, but do not chew the cud. Not only are they not fit for consumption, their carcasses should not even be touched (Deut 14:8).

Dietary laws are not understood to be arbitrary or insignificant. They are important as they are one of the ways that God's people are set apart from others. The writer of Deuteronomy reminds his readers that they "are the children of the Lord your God . . . chosen out of all the peoples on earth to be his people, his treasured possession" (Deut 14:1–2). The keeping of dietary laws is but one way to witness to the God of all creation.

Let's transition to the New Testament where there is a peculiar little story found in both the Gospels of Matthew and Mark that narrates the healing of a demoniac. Such stories are of obvious interest to me because if I wish to locate Satan, I may want to learn something about the way Satan and his army of demons conduct themselves—especially around the Jewish messiah. Mark 5 reads:

> They came to the other side of the sea, to the country of the Gerasenes. And when he had stepped out of the boat, immediately a man out of the tombs with an unclean spirit met him. He lived among the tombs; and no one could restrain him any more, even with a chain; for he had often been restrained with shackles and chains, but the chains he wrenched apart, and the shackles he broke in pieces; and no one had the strength to subdue him. Night and day among the tombs and on the mountains he was always howling and bruising himself with stones. When he saw Jesus from a distance, he ran and bowed down before him; and he shouted at the top of his voice, "What have you to do with me, Jesus, Son of the Most High God? I abjure you by God, do not torment me." For he had said to him, "Come out of the man, you unclean spirit!" [*What a strange way to phrase those last two sentences: Did Jesus*

*scream that from a distance and then the demoniac ran to him?
Also, notice how the demons are urging Jesus not to torment them
and are invoking the name of God to plead mercy. There appears to
be both fear and hope within the demons themselves.*] Then Jesus
asked him, "What is your name?" He replied, "My name is Legion;
for we are many." He begged him earnestly not to send them out
of the country. [*As it is lovely this time of year. Seriously though, is
this not a strange request? They are sort of saying, "We know you
are about to exorcize us, but we do really like this area." Weird.*]
Now there on a hillside a great herd of swine was feeding; and the
unclean spirits begged him, "Send us into the swine; let us enter
them." [*Even weirder.*] So he gave them permission. [*Weirdest thing
yet.*] And the unclean spirits came out and entered the swine; and
the herd, numbering about two thousand, rushed down the steep
bank into the sea and were drowned into the sea.

I love this story. It is just so, at the risk of being blatantly repetitive, weird.
Let's look at the facts of the story: some guy is possessed, endowing him
with superhero strength (demonic possession is the ultimate steroid);
Jesus gets out of a boat and attempts to heal him of the demons; the demons beg Jesus, by God, not to torment them or send them out of the
country, but to send them into some neighboring pigs; Jesus complies
and gives them permission to enter the pigs; and then the pigs run off an
embankment into the sea and drown.

Moral of the story?

No idea.

When the swine herdsman sees what happens he starts telling the
townspeople, who immediately ask Jesus to leave. They can hardly be
blamed. Jesus just sent two thousand pigs into the ocean to die. Somebody's
livelihood just tanked. How do you explain that to the wife?

"Honey, the Son of God allowed some demons to possess our pigs
and they killed themselves."

"Well," asks the bewildered missus, "why did he do that?"

"You know those Jews honey, they sure hate pigs."

At least when Terry Bradshaw kills a pig he feeds the homeless with
them. That's right, Terry Bradshaw created a movement called "Pigs for
Jesus." Despite the fact that Jesus was Jewish and would not have eaten
pigs, though he clearly has no aversion to sending demons into them,
Bradshaw raises them to feed the poor.

Some theologians and apologists claim that Jesus' sending of the demons into the swine was an indictment against the local people. The locals were unconcerned with the demoniac and they didn't care that he was healed. The only thing they appeared to be concerned with, so goes the argument, was their own property.

Such an interpretation, it seems, misses the point altogether. From this brief story alone, no one in the twenty-first century has the slightest idea what anyone was thinking or how they reacted to this cured demoniac. Rather the point is this: if Jesus has the power to exorcise demons, why send them into the pigs at all? Why not just send them to the abyss and be done with it? Why target someone's livelihood? This is not about wealth and prosperity, but survival. Only an affluent person with access to three to four meals a day, who has never had to rely on livestock for their survival, would be so condescending as to suggest that these people were simply greedy. I imagine if you were to read this text in any of the so-called third-world countries you would read it differently.

I'm guessing since Legion is referred to as unclean it was permissible to send them into unclean animals—these are animals, by the way, that we have only recently discovered to be highly intelligent creatures. Their level of intelligence is that of a small human child (anthropocentricism aside, that greatly trumps most dogs and many non-human primates). They are highly social and, if given the option, will gravitate toward a clean environment. They are also very close to us in terms of genetics. Their DNA is similar enough to ours that despite some religious traditions refusal to consume them, we can still harvest certain pig body parts (heart valves, skin, and kidneys) in order to replace those same parts of our body that need repair. Perhaps the reason various religious traditions such as Judaism, Islam, and Christianity continue to think of the pig as a dirty animal, often associated with demonology, is simply because they are so much like us.

This also raises fascinating questions in regards to demonic possession of nonhuman animals. In chapter 2 we learned about Cindy Jacob's demon-possessed cat. According to the story of Jesus and Legion, an exorcist can allow demons to enter nonhuman animals. Why this is allowed I'm not sure, unless it is simply the case that they have to go somewhere. In the case with Legion, did the demons drown or just the pigs? I'm guessing the answer would be just the pigs. So where did the demons go? Did they inhabit some crustaceans or cephalopods? Are they still swimming the seas looking for a lone diver to inhabit? Was the jellyfish that stung me possessed? What are they doing?

When I was in my early teens I attended a church camp where some of the ministers claimed that one of the young girls, a daughter of a pastor, was possessed by demons. The counselors and pastors at the camp made us vacate the sanctuary while they attempted to exorcize the demons from the little girl. We were told to leave because once the demons got out, they would look for someone else to possess. The next day about half of the campers refused to go back in the sanctuary as they couldn't convince us that those demons were not still on the loose.

The next year I remember someone asking if we should bring pigs. You know, just in case.

MR. PRESIDENT, WHO'S YOUR DADDY?

Let us pause in wonderment as the kings contrive an image of their god.
—Daniel Berrigan

There are numerous passages in the New Testament that talk about the Devil and his demons. I hope to mention some of those throughout the remainder of the book. There is, however, one more passage that I feel may be appropriate as I embark on this quest to locate Satan. It is Luke 4:5–7//Matt 4:8–9, with a slight nod to Revelation 13.

Revelation 13 is probably a tip-off and may say something about my deeply embedded anarchistic sensibilities. I'm captivated by the imagery of the blasphemous beast being "given authority over every tribe and people and language and nation" and how "all the inhabitants of the earth will worship it" (Rev 13:7–8). It just sounds far more interesting than the rather innocuous ring of free market capitalism backed by those nations with the military power to enforce it. I think the Book of Revelation is a wonderful political diatribe against the principalities and powers that constitute this world, and, to be honest, my search for Satan should include fieldtrips to the White House, Harvard Law School, and Disneyland. Unfortunately, rich and powerful people have little use for such conversations; they are far too busy running the world. I'm just going to have to hope that Satan is spreading himself a bit thin these days and is open to other venues of possible demonic corruption. Given that I have spent the last fifteen or so years of my life in numerous university settings, I am pretty confident that the Devil is capable of pulling off this feat.

The text that interests me the most is Luke 4:5–7. It reminds us that there is a strong strand of Gospel teaching that places all nations under the province of Satan. To illustrate this teaching, I keep in my office two lovely works of art by Gustave Dore. Hanging side by side is an illustration of Jesus and Satan standing on top of a high cliff with Satan showing Jesus all the kingdoms of the world, while the next illustration is that of the fallen and decimated Babylon. Occasionally a student will ask what they represent. Now that the poor unsuspecting student has taken the bait, I read to them out of the Gospel of Luke:

> Then the devil led him up and showed him in an instant all the kingdoms of the world. [*Note: ALL THE KINGDOMS*] And the devil said to him, "To you I will give their glory and all this authority; for it has been given over to me, and I give it to anyone I please. If you, then, will worship me, it will all be yours." Jesus answered him, "It is written, 'Worship the Lord your God and serve only him.'" (Luke 4:5–8)

There are a few things worthy of note in this passage. First of all, this temptation occurs in between two other temptations. After a long fast, Satan tempts Jesus to turn rocks into bread. When Jesus declines on this very intriguing possibility, Satan tempts him to jump off the top of the temple so that the angels would catch him. "On their hands they will bear you up," Satan tells him, "so that you will not dash your foot against a stone" (Luke 4:11).

When I was a kid, this latter story really confused me. I thought to myself, Why would Jesus need angels to catch him? If Satan can fly, surely the second person of the triune God can fly, too. I mean, the guy walks on water, through walls, and disappears into thin air. I'm not sure why this requires that much of a stretch of imagination. When I expressed my theological observations to one of my Sunday school teachers I was quickly reprimanded for confusing Jesus with Superman.

"Well, if Jesus can't fly," I pitifully, but honestly, reasoned, "I have to say, Superman seems much cooler."

I knew as soon as I uttered those words I was going to get in a lot trouble. My Nazarene church family did not suffer sacrilege lightly.

Tangent aside.

After noting where this temptation takes place, it's also crucial to observe that Satan's claim to ownership, despite his being a reputable liar, is never challenged. Jesus clearly seems to accept it without argument. This clears the way for a third point: Satan does not only claim ownership, he says that is has been "given" to him. It is safe to assume that it has been given to him by the one who ordains such authorities: God the Father. This, of course, raises a whole host of issues, primarily: if it is the case that all of the kingdoms of the world are under the control of Satan it is only because God, as in the case of Job, has handed such authority over to him. Satan, in a theologically dubious kind of way, offers to give it back—at least to the Son. Of course, it does not come cheap. In order for Jesus to have all of the kingdoms of the world he has to worship Satan. Jesus passes on the opportunity to rule the world—at least in the way the world rules the world. Which leads me to my final point of this brief passage: Satan gives the keys to the world's kingdoms to those he chooses.

"I give it to anyone I please," claims the Devil.

I imagine the logical conclusion to this passage is a bitter pill for many of us to swallow. Our democratically idealized ears must find such a notion repulsive, especially since *we* are the government. If Satan really is the prince of the air and has the power to give control to those who worship him, then this whole finding Satan thing may be a bit more complicated than I thought. After all, if you have ever voted, you may be conspiring with the object of my search.

This raises some genuinely provocative questions about the powers ordained by God. Though all forms of authority may, ultimately, be under the rule of God, this ability of Satan to give to whom Satan chooses renders this a bit messy. Is it God or Satan who places believers and/or nonbelievers in power? Did God or Satan orchestrate the placement of two Roman emperors, Nero and Diocletian (among others), responsible for so many Christian deaths? Did God or Satan place Pontius Pilate in power in order to make sure that Jesus suffered death? Was it God or Satan who convinced millions of Germans to democratically elect the most tyrannical leader in the twentieth century, Adolph Hitler? Did God or Satan put in power the likes of Truman, Mao, Stalin, Nixon, Pinochet, Ho Chi Minh, General Ky, Gorbachev, Reagan, Thatcher, Hussein, Castro, Bush,

Clinton, Bush Pt. II, Bin-Laden, Mugabe, Blair, and Obama? According to Luke, the one thing all these leaders have in common is the idea that Satan gives power to those who worship him.

Take that up with your conscience the next time you vote.

I'm aware this is a rather scandalous interpretation of this passage. If it is outrageous, maybe it is only because it is true. I'm only trying to take Scripture seriously. I'm not sure why I cannot take this passage any more literally than how I'm told I have to take passages on sex, money, and lying literally. Yet this passage seems to go largely ignored—even by the most devout believer in Satan. I've heard a wide assortment of responses from various ministers, professors, priests, and theologians about this passage, many of which have not given the "Devil his due." To give you an idea of some of those responses I am including six of them, many of which were repeated by numerous interviewees, that I found to be fairly representative of how many people understand this passage.

Response Number One:

"This is not to be taken literally," claimed an Episcopalian priest. "This story symbolically reminds us that God's kingdom is not of this world."

"But Jesus already said his kingdom is not of this world," I responded. "Why would we need a symbolic reminder of something Jesus plainly stated?"

"To reinforce what we know to be the truth by more than words alone," he explained. "Words are easy, simple, they come so cheap."

"But those are the words of Jesus. Are you saying that Jesus does not mean what he says?"

"No, no. Only that symbolism often carries the weight that a literal truth could never bear."

At first I found this to be relatively profound, until I realized he was just keeping the door open to vote Democrat.

Response Number Two:

"How do we even know this really happened?" laughed a Unitarian minister. "If Jesus was really up there on that hill with Satan, how would anyone know to write this story down?"

"You realize," I asked, "you're being no help whatsoever, right?"

"That's what you get for asking someone who doesn't consider any text canonical."

Except, I guess, for the entire canon produced by the Enlightenment.

Response Number Three:

"Do you know," asked the Methodist minister, "when you are about to do something bad, and you have that whole angel on one shoulder thing with a demon on the other?"

"Not really."

Oblivious to my answer he continued, "Well, this is that same sort of situation."

"So," I asked, "Jesus is up there talking to himself?"

"Sure, why not? We do it all the time, and Jesus really is human, so why not? This being the case, this image of him on the mountain debating with himself over whether or not he should conquer the kingdoms of this world in a way that many Jews thought the messiah would—through military conquest—reveals his own inner struggle with how he was attempting to deal with what many were expecting of him. It was an existential crisis of sorts."

Did he really just say "existential"?

Jesus may be many things to lots of different people, but the one thing he cannot be is interested in the self-aggrandizing yet thoroughly self-negating world of existentialism. Sorry, it's not allowed.

Response Number Four:

"Jesus," stated another Unitarian minister, "was very likely hallucinating."

Why do I keep asking Unitarians what they think?

Response Number Five:

"God wants to place into power people who will do the bidding of the Lord," claimed a twenty-five year veteran of the Presbyterian pulpit. "Yet, because we have free will, we are influenced by Satan to sometimes make the wrong choice. Not always, or as a rule, but certainly as often as we get it right. That is why it is so important that we pray ceaselessly before we vote."

"But if the decision ultimately goes to Satan, why does it matter how much we pray?"

"Because," he told me, "we can trump the will of Satan whenever our prayer life informs our voting practices."

At first I found this to be relatively profound, until I realized he was just keeping the door open to vote Republican.

Response Number Six:

A Church of God preacher informed me, "You have to take this story in context. You see, at the time, all of the kingdoms of this world were demonic. They were under Satan's control. Once Jesus became king of all the nations, through his resurrection, only those countries that refuse to recognize Jesus as their Lord and Savior remain under the power of Satan."

"That's very Constantinian of you."

"Very what?" he asked.

"Nothing. But could you tell me which countries you think are currently under the power of Satan?"

"Well, I would have to say most of them. Afghanistan. Iraq. Kuwait. Cuba. India. Switzerland. France. Most of Europe, I guess. Vietnam is still communist, right? And, you know, God is doing some wonderful things in Africa, but there are still lots of areas in need of evangelization there, too."

"What about the United States?" I asked.

"Well, she comes and goes in terms of whose authority she's under. Sometimes she's under the power of Satan, and sometimes she's not. It all depends. I don't want to get all political on you, as I know that may make you feel uncomfortable."

"You just chalked up most of the world as being demonic; I don't think you need to worry about my feelings now."

We shared a good laugh.

He continued, "Well, let's just say that in our recent past, it is safe to say that for a number of years the United States was under the authority of God, but obviously all of that has now changed."

"Why do you think it has changed?" I asked.

"It could be that we have become too complacent, and that God is now challenging us by placing a person in authority that is going to remind us of what is really important. Satan is up there on that very hill right now, Capitol Hill you might say, asking us if we are going to worship him. We can only return God's rule to this country by returning this nation to its once former glorious self. We have to get back to a time when Christians were in positions of authority, when prayer was allowed in schools, when courthouses could display the Ten Commandments without fear of the ACLU, when—"

"When white people owned black people?" I interrupted.

I'm always baffled as to people's response to this passage. Even the most Satan-fearing literalist likes to somehow explain this passage away. Of all the countless people I talked to, many of whom found Satan under every rock, very few of them understood Satan as the present ruler of all kingdoms—if by all kingdoms we include the United States. Why do most

Christians struggle with the idea that Satan's ownership of all nations in-cludes the United States of America? Despite the many wonderful things many people in this nation have accomplished, we still cannot ignore the fact that our presence here resulted in the complete decimation of the Native American populace. The so-called Founders were deistic slave owners, some of whom forcibly took carnal pleasure (as my grandmother would call it) out on those they owned. In the twentieth century, a century in which the majority of political positions were held by Christians (as is still the case), those gentiles who lorded their power over us determined who sat where on a bus, who were able to use certain water fountains and toilets, who dined at certain restaurants, who were able to swim in public swimming pools, who were able to vote, and where certain people could and could not attend school. Certainly segregation, as primarily defended in the 60s by morally and politically conservative Christians, was not an exercise in holy virtue.

But, hey, at least we had prayer in schools.

My bet on this passage? I think if there were ever an indication that Scripture should be taken literally, it is this passage in Luke and Matthew. The empirical evidence behind our history of monarchies, empires, and nation-states is more than enough evidence to suggest that there is a real "beast" behind governmental authorities. If you are looking for an experi-ence that genuinely proves the existence of the Devil, then it has to be the manner in which nations lord their rule over us as they persist in acting as our benefactors (Luke 22:25). Speaking for myself, if there is ever a mo-ment I am tempted to believe in demonic possession, it is when Christians reflect back on a "time when the United States was a godly nation," when white Christians could call African-Americans "niggers" without fear of retribution, when women "kept their place" in the house, and when a prominent white televangelist could discuss the "Jewish problem" over prayer with a corrupt president. Yes, for many Christians, it was a regular golden age back when we had prayer in school.

Of course, after segregation became illegal, there was a surge in the creation of private Protestant "Christ-centered" schools. I guess this was an attempt to make sure nothing happened to school prayer.

Well, that or something to do with keeping their schools free of black people.

Which, of course, is but one reason why Revelation refers to Babylon as a whore: "And on her forehead was written a name, a mystery: 'Babylon the Great, mother of whores, and of earth's abominations'" (Rev 17:5). I hope those fine men and women who work the streets, as well as those at the disposal of many prominent evangelists and politicians, do not take offense at such a comment. This passage is not about selling our time and bodies for money. We all do that. This text, I think, and much of Revelation for that matter, is about the judgment that is going to be wrought on those nations who do not exercise mercy and justice toward the poor, the widowed, the orphan, the alien, the immigrant (illegal or not), and the stranger. Revelation affirms Satan's claims of ownership over all nations, and argues, as do the Psalms, Isaiah, and Matthew, that God will judge the nations and separate us as a nation from the nations, based on our ability to enact his cruciform love (Matt 25:32).

The Gospels of Luke and Matthew, as well as John's Revelation, reinforce the notion that Satan's influence is behind all rulers and authorities, yet I wonder if I cannot locate a more specific experience with these cosmic powers that Paul mentions. If all those I spoke with in the first two chapters are correct, perhaps I will find the Devil amidst the Satanists, fortune-tellers, pagans, druids, and Unitarians.

That's right. I said it.

Unitarians.

4 DENYING THE DEVIL

The Devil is, historically, the God of any people that one personally dislikes.

—Aleister Crowley

The world is all the richer for having a devil in it, so long as we keep our foot on his neck.

—William James

In the first two chapters, I reflected on conversations that assumed the existence of Satan as well as the standard demonic fare that follows such a belief. Despite not being able to physically locate Satan, I found myself surrounded by people who were as sure of his existence as they were of God's existence. Satan, it would seem, is as active in this world as the One who created him. In this chapter, I will examine a few groups that some of my interviewees in chapters 1 and 2 claimed were satanic. If I am seeking evidence for the existence of Satan, then it only makes sense to examine those who others claim to be satanic. What renders my strategy so convoluted, however, is the fact that many of the people within this chapter do not actually believe in Satan's existence. Perhaps, for those in the first two chapters, this is what makes them even more dangerous. This chapter includes conversations with a Unitarian minister, a druid cleric, a pagan shamanist-healer, and a few Satanists. Most, if not all of these people would consider themselves to be humanists—hence, demonic to a number of people of certain religious traditions. Though many of them deny the existence of Satan, I did not allow foreknowledge of such a denial to deter me in my search. After all, sometimes the best way to find something is to look in what you originally assumed to be the wrong place.

UNITARIAN UNIVERSALISM:
THE BORING-ALITY OF EVIL

Unitarianism has a great noble history. It's about a strong affirmation of the oneness of God, only it just got eaten up by a kind of liberal humanism, and as a result, I think it's an extraordinarily uninteresting group.

—Stanley Hauerwas

Self-begot, self-raised, By our own quick'ning power . . .

—Satan (John Milton, *Paradise Lost*)

Unitarians are my favorite heretics.

By that I'm not implying that Unitarianism is my favorite heresy; I bestow that particular honor to Pelagianism. I think a little Pelagianism would be good for the church.

It never hurts to try harder.

I am only saying that if I had to choose—you know, the whole gun-to-the-head scenario—I would rather hangout with a Unitarian than, say, a Gnostic. This is quite difficult, of course, because if Harold Bloom is correct then most people in the United States are Gnostics.[1]

Thanks to Bloom for accurately conflating the issue.

Though the Unitarian church can trace its history through a corpus of work dating back to the early church (though not really defined and developed until the seventeenth century), its blossoming, it seems, can only occur in a culture predisposed to spiritualize everything and make knowledge an interior phenomenon. If this is the case, it may not be possible to hangout with a Unitarian who is not Gnostic.

Oh well. They're still a good time.

Based on numerous conversations I have had with Unitarian Universalists, I was not terribly keen on the idea of asking them about their thoughts on Satan. I was convinced that their theology, or lack thereof, would not be very helpful for my particular pursuit. For the most part, this was true. The Unitarian Universalist Church, however, does not dictate what people have to believe in order to belong to their church. They claim to be open to everyone. They consider themselves a creedless

---

1. See Bloom, *American Religion*.

body of people who, despite their non-creedal nature, are loosely bound together by a number of principles. These principles, to summarize, include a general concern for the dignity and rights of all people. Overall, however, a good Unitarian would never dictate what another Unitarian must believe or not believe (except you cannot believe in creeds because they dictate what one must believe), leaving me with the possibility of finding some divergent accounts on the Prince of Darkness.

I decided to meet with the local Unitarian minister in order to talk about a variety of things—specifically if he had any information on the whereabouts of Satan. I also wanted an excuse to discuss their dogmatic refusal to be dogmatic, their love for all religions (despite their refusal to accept any of them as true), as well as adultery. Well, that last bit certainly wasn't the plan, but it happened anyway.

When I arrived at the church I was grateful it didn't look like your typical non-denominational warehouse. It was rather avant-garde in design—white, and oddly shaped, but with a post-modern kind of feel. It was by no means a thing of beauty, as I'm all about the gothic look when it comes to churches, but it was certainly better than the norm.

As I approached the front door, I noticed I had to ring a doorbell. Despite having seven cars in the parking lot, the front door was locked. Not only was it locked, it had a sign stating they will not open the door for strangers.

So much for not being a "members only" kind of crowd.

If you want to get inside the church, the sign read, you have to schedule an appointment. Good thing I called ahead.

The resident minister opened the door. He was probably in his mid-fifties with a pretty killer hairline. He showed me around the church and we chose the sanctuary for our discussion space. It was a very small, but lovely sanctuary. He informed me that they have about eighty-five participants a week, which in the Protestant-dominated world that is south central Kentucky, was more than I imagined. Throughout the sanctuary there were beautiful stained-glass paintings depicting images associated with the world's major religions. The chief symbols for Judaism, Taoism, Buddhism, Islam, Christianity, and Hinduism were all present. I found this to be incredibly ironic given that, from my understanding, there were no Jews, Taoists, Buddhists, Muslims, Christians, or Hindus attending the church. I could not understand the need to celebrate these other religious groups' rather exclusive identities that, by the Unitarian's very gathering, suggests a denial of their validity. Maybe I will find out later.

The minister is an ex-Catholic turned "general theist turned spiritual seeker." Such seeking led him to read Kerouac, Whitman, Emerson, and Twain. What he found most compelling about these authors is that "they all teach you that there is no answer outside of the answer that you must find for yourself."

I admit to being confused about the intelligibility of such a claim. First of all, how would anyone know this to be true—at least in such a manner that you can make an objective claim about the non-objective reality of subjective reality? Second, how is the doctrine that you have to teach someone that "the only valid answers are the answers you find on your own" not a self-defeating form of indoctrination? Apparently you must be taught that only the answers you find within yourself are legitimate answers. If this is the case, should I not reject a theory based on the premise? If I didn't come up with it, how can anything learned on my own really be my own? Basically, I guess, Whitman, Emerson, Twain, Rand, and other "like-minded individuals" have to teach me how to be an individual.

Are there any Enlightenment conceptions of individuality not mired in nonsense?

After graduating from Brandeis University, my new friend eventually made his way to Andover Newton Theological Seminary in order to gain a Masters of Divinity degree, which, I am guessing, will better enable him to lead others to their own self-truths.

Back to this in a moment.

It's time to get to the reason for my visit. Unfortunately, when the minister informed me that in all of his years of preaching and teaching he had never even referenced Satan, I realized I was probably barking up the wrong tree. I asked him to explain the absence of Satan in his sermons and conversations.

"Well," he told me, "I don't think people find it a useful term because, and I'm just guessing, but my guess is that it fits in the same kind of category as Santa Claus: something that doesn't exist."

Excellent.

I am such a fan of anyone who can so breezily jettison, as nonsense, what so many people believe. This makes for a far more engaging conversation.

He continued, "It is a personification of something that does exist. Santa Claus is the personification of the generous impulse, I suppose, and Satan being the personification of the destructive impulse, or the rebellious impulse, or however you want to define evil. That is coming from the humanist tradition, the humanist understanding of Satan, and most of the people you will find here are humanist. The other way of understanding Satan, of course, is something outside of us, something created . . . I don't know how many people here are familiar with the Genesis story, but I do inform people here of their Christian and Jewish roots so they can understand that which they come from."

This was, for a number of reasons, a fascinating claim: one, this group that claims a Judeo-Christian heritage may or may not be familiar with the "Genesis story" (where are the fundamentalists when you need them?); two, Satan represents an impulse—though such a reading is completely absent from any canonical text; and three, point two doesn't matter because for Unitarians there is no canonical text. What you can learn from the prophets, the Gospels, or anything else in Scripture, is on par with what you can learn from the Romanticists or the Beat Poets. If it makes sense to you, then you should learn from it. As he informed me, since they are without a creed, there can be no communal understanding of any authoritative scripture. "Coming from a non-creedal tradition," he claimed, "there is nothing for anyone to believe, in terms of a belief system, in order to become a Unitarian Universalist."

"How is the defining of one's self," I asked, "or, you know, 'We are non-creedal, and we should have no belief system other than the belief system that we should have no belief system' not a belief system?"

He thought for a moment and then, oddly enough, offered me some pamphlets on the Unitarian Universalist Church. I say "oddly enough" because if there is nothing one must think or believe to be a Unitarian Universalist, do I really need literature explaining to me that there is nothing I must think or believe to be a Unitarian Universalist?

After handing me the pamphlets, I said, "This, to me, seems just as dogmatic as saying, 'Here's the Nicene Creed, memorize it and live by it.'"

"Well," he hesitantly offered, "it may seem that way . . . but it's not."

I looked at him to see if he was going to elaborate on his response, which, in all fairness, was not much of a response, when he began reading, or I should say *reciting*, to me the various principles of his non-creedal church. When I asked him if you have to believe in these principles to be a Unitarian he said, "No, these are merely basic precepts that many of us agree on, but you do not have to agree with them, or even have an agreed understanding of their interpretation, to be a part of this church."

I pushed him a little more on what it means to be a Unitarian. I asked him numerous questions: What truly demarcates a Unitarian from a non-Unitarian? Am I not a Unitarian because I am a Trinitarian? If not, how is being Unitarian somehow less dogmatic than being Trinitarian? Can I pretty much believe anything I want as long as I do not think that, say, Judaism, Islam, or Christianity are possibly correct?

It was on this last point that I found his position most telling. For instance, he claimed that it is permissible for a Unitarian Universalist to believe in Satan, if he or she likes, but it is certainly not necessary. He told me that the reason they have images of all of these religions in their sanctuary is to allow his congregants to understand that there are various paths, all of which lead to their own truths, and, therefore, they do not want to push any of them on anyone.

"But how is that not incredibly intolerant?" I asked.

My question caught him off-guard as a good Unitarian prides his or her self on being tolerant. He asked for clarification.

I told him the moment one makes the claim that any and all religions are just as valid as any other religions (the gist of religious pluralism) then you have placed yourself in a bind. "Even though it appears to be very inclusivistic, very tolerant, at root it is entirely exclusivistic," I argued. "What it is really saying is that Judaism, Islam, and Christianity, for example, are wrong."

In a very offended tone he asked, "Wrong? How do you get that?"

"Well, try telling a devout Muslim that their path is of equal validity to that of a Buddhist, or that a Hasidic Jew is on a path that is just as truthful as the Christian path. The narratives that are Christianity, Islam, and Judaism make claims about the way the world is, and what you are saying is that they are incorrect, that Jesus is not the only way to the Father, that Allah is not the one true God, and that the God of Israel is not the God of the universe who is going to punish people for worshipping false gods."

"Well, when you put it that way, then I guess we are saying that, but I wouldn't put it that way."

"But you already have put it that way," I said. "I don't know how else you can tell a Jew that Taoism is just as legitimate a path to the truth as the Torah without implying that Judaism is wrong. Plus, isn't the claim that all paths lead to the same goal just as much of a meta-narrative as the claim that Jesus is the only way to the Father? I don't see any difference."

Like so many of my other interviews, once they start heading south ministers quickly look at their watches. He informed me that he had another meeting coming up, but unlike other people I interviewed who wished to dispense of me, this very kind soul asked me if I would like to continue our conversation outside, and then on to lunch. Do you now understand why Unitarians are my favorite heretics? Despite their incredible propensity for philosophical naiveté, they are just so, well, nice.

As we sat outside, we carried on our conversation that did, in case you are wondering, come back to the subject of Satan. But I think this part of the conversation is actually important to his concluding thoughts on the non-ontological status of Satan, so I'll stay with it.

I continued pushing him on what it meant to be a Unitarian. I offered an example of the sort of clear demarcation between certain religious communities. I explained how, for instance, as a Mennonite I'm not allowed to engage in a number of activities ranging from violence, to stealing, to adultery. Once I commit one of these acts, I can be placed under the ban by my church. This is what the Catholic Church refers to as excommunication. Just as Catholics do not divorce or practice abortion, Mennonites are a community of people who do not (or are not supposed to) war, steal, or cheat on their spouses (among many other things). I explained that despite the immediate gratification or assuagement of certain feelings, regardless of what sort of good can come from "that little lady I may be eying," if I am married I am not allowed to act on such an impulse. If I do, I risk no longer being a Mennonite.

"So I guess" I told him, "what I was asking when I was asking what makes a Unitarian a Unitarian was not to promote such a stark contrast, but I myself know if I'm engaging in an activity that places into question whether or not I am still a Mennonite. Because the community has defined that over me, and I am wondering, and I hope this is not too off-putting, but . . . can a Unitarian commit adultery and still be a Unitarian?"

Very significant pause.

When he finally did reply, it was with a question for me. "Can a human being be fallible and still be a human being?"

Believing his response to have missed my point I answered, "Oh, well, that's part of what it means to be human, I guess . . . that and something to do with our genetic makeup. I guess what I'm asking, with such a question, is that I know as a Mennonite my community places certain barriers on what I can and cannot do in order for me to fully understand what I am saying when I say I am a Mennonite. So, I want to know if a Unitarian is still a Unitarian if they commit adultery."

An even longer pause this time followed by yet another question for me.

"Are you still a human being if you have fallibility?"

Realizing he is just dodging my question, I asked, "So, 'yes' is what you are saying?"

"Well," he protested, "I am certainly not going to answer that question 'yes' or 'no' because it's a 'gotcha' question."

"It could be a gotcha question, and if so, I'm not sure why that is a bad thing. I'm just attempting find out if there is anything that sets a Unitarian apart from a non-Unitarian that may be recognizable to other Unitarians—as well as non-Unitarians. I mean, even if you claim to be creedless and non-institutional, there is still a body of people that claim to be Unitarian, and I want to know how that is different from, say, the Amish."

I was thinking he was going to answer with something funny like, "We have zippers on our pants." Instead, in a very frustrated manner, he claimed that what makes them different from the Amish is "we don't have a creed."

For some reason, when I think of creedal traditions the Amish are not the first that come to my mind.

"I still do not see," I insisted, "how that isn't creedal."

"Well," he explained, "maybe because it's your worldview that includes things that are creedal and—"

"Maybe," I interrupted, "you should have a creed and then you guys wouldn't commit adultery."

That came out of nowhere.

Normally, I would take full responsibility for blurting out such a rude comment, but I honestly think it has more to do with the person who directed my master's thesis.

I will not say his name, but it rhymes with Schmauerwas.

Amazingly enough, even after my unwarranted cheap shot he still wanted to converse with me. We agreed that the creeds certainly do not act as a deterrent against adultery. Apparently, people will find a way to poke around in other people's bodies with or without Nicea. At least with the creeds, however, you have the resources that tell you that you should not poke around in other people's bodies. If you are your own authority, as within the Unitarian church, I am not sure you could ever know that adultery is problematic. It could only be problematic if you personally decided that it was problematic. For the Unitarian, it is certainly not sinful to commit adultery. To be able to name something as a sin requires a grammatical framework and a shared, demarcating way of life. Akin to their more theologically orthodox Episcopalian brothers and sisters, I'm not even sure it's possible for them to sin. Of course, Jesus does say, "Go and sin no more." I guess they figured out how to do it.

Or, not do it.

Knowing this was not going to get us anywhere, I redirected the conversation back to Satan. I was discussing how in the New Testament Satan seems to be far more than the personification of some rebellious force. I was talking about numerous passages in the Gospels, the Pauline literature, as well as Revelation where Satan seems to be an actual being. I asked him who he thought Jesus was talking to when Jesus and Satan were up on top of the hill discussing the fate of all the kingdoms of the world.

"Jesus," he told me, "had a remarkable passion for understanding the nature of humanity and wanting to reconcile humanity to God. Part of his discipline, similar to the discipline of the Buddha, was fasting. He would pray and he would fast. Both of those things have physiological ramifications, and neurological ramifications that are . . . and I am not a reductionist nor a materialist, but I do think the body and the mind and the soul are all connected, and if you fast and pray then it seems to me that there are going to be things that happen in your mind that are going to bring you out of yourself. Now whether this is what people call a mystical experience or what people call a delusional experience is up to how you interpret things. I think when you have that much of a passion to live a good life, to live a life in accordance with God who you see as your father, that is going to create a sensibility that we can talk about in abstract terms but he can experience in terms of the body. So, whether Satan is actually there or Satan materializes as a manifestation of his mental state because of his prayer and fasting, I don't know the answer to that. To me it is not as interesting as the dialogue that he has with Satan where he clarifies his values."

That last bit of dialogue was worth the wait. I have had countless ministers and priests say something very similar on this passage. That is,

Jesus was simply battling with himself, fighting his own inner demons so to speak, wrestling with the knowledge that, if he wanted to, he could conquer the kingdoms of this world in a way that the world would understand—through force. Jesus was simply on that mountain talking to himself about his possible options.

I understand this position. I really do. However, this minister is the first I have encountered who pointed out that a radical prayer life, coupled with fasting, can make one hallucinate. Due to his fervent prayer life and lack of food, Jesus was possibly having, speculated the minister, an out of body experience that made the presence of an alternative reality to the course of God seem very real.

At least the good minister was not being, as he claimed, reductionistic.

Of course, much of what he said is true. Fasting for lengthy periods of time can cause hallucinations. Much of what passes for mysticism in the Christian tradition occurs precisely due to the practices of fasting and continual prayer. This does not render such experiences as worthless or as meaninglessness; rather, these practices often function as the pathways to such experiences. A means to an end, you could say. Just because you can explain how the means leads to the end does not mean that the end, or the means, is illegitimate.

To suggest that Jesus was suffering from delusions, or for that matter may have even been a bit off his rocker, is not entirely farfetched. Look at everything he taught: give away all your money (or at least half of it); if someone hits you, let them hit you again; if someone asks for your shirt, give them your coat, too; if your right hand offends you, cut it off; if your eyes cause you to sin, pluck them out; hate your mother and father; love your enemies; pray for those who persecute you; do not tell lies; be as righteous as the Pharisees; and, among many other things, do not commodify your religion. All of these things are absolutely insane because there is not a single one of them anyone can reconcile with the common sense that constitutes our daily reality—which, I am guessing, is why he had to be killed. A person like that is too much of a threat to common sense, to the basic order of things. He may give people crazy ideas like sharing possessions and refusing to participate in war. So the fact that he may have talked to himself on occasion may not be that much of a stretch.

While I was trying to process the minister's claims, he immediately directed the conversation toward existentialism (ugh—Unitarians and freshly minted MDiv Methodists love existentialism). The fact that we went from Jesus transcending and talking to himself to French philosophers such as Camus and Sartre is not that much of a leap. For this particular Unitarian, Jesus was just one of the forerunners of existentialism. Jesus on the mountain, like Siddhartha under the Bodhi tree, was having an existential crisis about who he was, what he was called to be, and how he stood in relation to the world. To literalize such a crisis, he told me, would only miss the point of our individual search for purpose and meaning.

With so much talk about our own path to salvation, meaning, and purpose, I asked on what grounds such a search takes place given that there appears to be no authority other than the authority you declare for yourself, which, in turn, dictates the pursuit of one's salvation. I understand how critics of traditional religions suggest that religions are nothing more than organized ventures into self-fulfillment, but how are the Unitarians any different?

Trying to work this out I asked, "Without some sort of outside canon the only canon you end up with is yourself, which is very much a general precept of the Enlightenment. This notion seems to be at the heart of the Unitarian Universalist Church, that you become your own best authority."

"I think so," he responded.

"Yeah?"

"Yes, I think so," he responded.

We sat in silence for a few moments as I thought about such a claim. Finally, I let out a frustrated sigh and uttered, "Ah, the tyranny of the individual self. You see, that frightens me."

As if he was attempting to comfort me he said, "Well, you become your own authority . . . because you're all you got."

I sat there and let his Kantian cliché wash over me.

I felt so dirty.[2]

I confessed my true fear, "You see, I become a nihilist when I hear that."

2. Kantian stains are hard to get out. I suggest pre-treating them with the work of Alasdair MacIntyre. If Kant has soiled you theologically, multiple treatments from various thinkers such as Søren Kierkegaard, Karl Barth, and John Milbank may be necessary.

Kant to Nietzsche makes perfect sense.

"Oh," he gently responded. Very philosophically he stated, "Now isn't that interesting?"

"Yeah."

"Huh. Well . . ."

"Yeah."

"You want to get lunch?" he asked.

"Sure."

We went to lunch and continued our conversation. I told him I thought some of the problems I was finding with the Unitarian Universalist Church could be resolved if they spent more time reading Feuerbach and Nietzsche. These two atheists, especially the latter, refused to deify humans in the absence of God. From the many, many different Unitarians I spoke with, as well as the several church services I attended, I felt as though there was some sort of sentimentalized version of Nietzsche's will to power at work. I continue to find that frightening.

I mean, talk about stepping into the abyss with a smile on your face.

Speaking of which—well, sort of—the fact that we talked about suicide was not lost on me. He told me that everyday we have to make a conscious decision as to whether or not there is something to get up for.

"That," I confessed, "seems terribly oppressive."

"Well," he responded, "it's . . . well . . . that's why you need faith."

Faith in what, I have no idea.

I should point out that lunch was excellent. As I sat there listening to him speak of his own authoritative self, and the need to find a reason within one's self to get up in the morning (since there can be no reason other than the reason you decide is a legitimate reason), I was left wondering if, for some people, a good meal is all one needs to keep going.

Would the prospect of a really ripe tomato coupled with mozzarella cheese doused in vinegar and basil get me through a Nietzschean night?

I don't know.

But we did dine like kings.

DRUIDIAN CAPITALISM

Every hour on the news we have business hour—every hour—it's sort of a hymn to capitalism.

—Tony Benn

God is dead, but has been resurrected as "Capital."

—Jeremy Carrette and Richard King

While still living in North Carolina, I was able to take advantage of a rather large, vibrant, and growing underground community of wiccans, pagans, and practitioners of the occult. Such activity is located in the Research Triangle Area where there are a large number of universities within a relatively small geographical area. I am not suggesting that universities are responsible for developing alternative religious habits, only that for many kids, if there is ever a time to experiment, it is during the secular world's version of *rumpsringa*.

Rumspringa means to "run around." It's the Amish practice of allowing their sixteen-year-old children the time and space to experience what the Amish refer to as the Devil's playground. During this time, Amish kids learn how to, first, properly shop (if you want to be "English" you have to know how to spend money). They purchase everything from cars to clothes to cell phones. All of these items contribute to the ultimate goal of being able to consume inordinate amounts of alcohol, pop pills, smoke weed, and have sex with people they don't even know.

It's college sans the expensive degree.

We should not, therefore, be surprised to find a significant amount of experimentation, even in regards to religious practices, when it comes to the "English" version of *rumspringa* known as college.

This particular interview was with a neo-druid priestess who lived in Greensboro, North Carolina. Due to Greensboro hosting five universities, it happens to be home to at least a few college-age witches, pagans, and other kids trying hard to rebel against mommy and daddy in the most shocking way a rich privileged white kid can rebel. In saying this, I do not mean to demean those who, upon stumbling upon these paths while in college, have dedicated their lives to Wicca or some form of paganism.

I'm only pointing out that there are certain patterns all animals tend to follow, and the human animal is no different. I'm sure Wicca is no better off having college-aged kids experiment with it for a few years than Christianity is when a failing metal, pop, or country music star decides to give their life to Jesus in order to procure musical engagements in large, well-paying churches.

As we began our conversation, I was a bit dismayed that most of her comments were purely reactionary. Every question I asked, regardless of the question, came back to how we are all destroying Gaia and how the structures established and perpetuated via the dominance of the male have resulted in the "materialized rape of the spiritual world." Now, had she talked about the materialized rape of the material world, I think I could have followed, and even agreed with her. But how does one materially rape the spiritual?

I could only conclude that she had been recently misreading Andrea Dworkin and Mary Daly.

Of course, I knew I was in trouble when the first thing she told me was that she was "spiritual, not religious."

Not trendy at all these druids, not trendy at all.

I decided not to vocalize my feelings. At least, not yet. I needed some information. I needed something different from the things I would find amidst my Christian brothers and sisters. Surely, a genuine honest-to-God neo-druid priestess would give me something of interest.

Alas, this was not to be the case.

I discovered that neither she, nor any of her druids-in-arms girlfriends, actually believed in the personification of evil—except in the sense of how humans abuse the earth. I appreciate the earth-friendly sentiment. I really do. Yet, this was disconcerting. I thought a good pagan could help me out in a time like this. I was raised believing that Satan loved witches and pagans, and yet, here they are, or at least a few of them, telling me they don't even believe in Satan. "As a matter of fact," she told me, "I would pretty much say we don't believe in most of what the Westernized world teaches."

Which was odd, because thus far all I had heard were "Westernized" teachings. Before I could suggest that her ideological indoctrination was about as far West as one could get, she started talking about a wedding ceremony she had recently performed. She was telling me how spiritually significant it was for everyone involved due to some Celtic wannabes beating drums "out of time, but in time with the rhythm of our true spiritual selves."

I confess I wanted to end the conversation right there (I was thinking I would rather suffer through an episode of *Friends* then spend another five minutes talking to her). And since she was not going to give me anything good on evil, as she did not believe in Satan (only "negative energy arising from our collectively altered sub-consciousness due to the contemptuous forces of group thought"—okay), I thought I would at least wrap up the conversation by finding out exactly how her particular form of faith made her different than any other person in our culture.

"So, what do you guys and gals actually believe?" I asked.

"That we are our own gods and goddesses. We are our own inner light that shines through when we answer only to the authority that is ourselves."

Was I experiencing déjà vu? Was she a Unitarian?

Either that or she was a prime example of what happens when North American Gnostics start doing yoga.

I asked her how she grounds authority in herself. What does that mean? How does one only answer to themselves in such a way that they can be sure they are not simply buying into our present cultural epoch that has constructed a deity out of the individual?

She informed me that it "happens through close attention to the rhythms discovered though the natural world. Our authority is our mother earth. It is to her that we come and to her we shall return. Our authority to ourselves is only truthful when we listen to her, as we are from her, and we are her."

"So, what exactly does that look like?" I asked. "What exactly does this mean in regards to how you actually live?"

"We live free of all things that would attempt to blind us to who we really are, of who we are supposed to be."

"Which is?"

"Free spiritual beings living in harmony with nature, who are at one with the forces of the universe."

I almost told her that I wanted to be a Jedi, too, but at this point I needed her to give me at least one answer that actually meant something. I just wanted one response that had some sort of pragmatic intelligibility.

Pressing on I asked, "Again, what does that look like?

"Well," as she pointed to herself, "I guess it looks like this." She was smiling, wearing her requisite love bead bracelets, crystal-laden hemp necklace, and a number of tattoos in fetishized foreign languages on her bare arms and legs, which were unshaven to prove that she would not sculpt herself in the image of men—unless such men own stores that carry bracelets, necklaces, crystals, or any other fashion wear commensurate with her "dissident" way of life.

I continued to push for a more precise response. "Well, what exactly," pointing to her, "is this?"

"What do you mean?" she asked.

"Okay, let me take a different approach. Just answer this question: What did you do yesterday? Just give me a moment-by-moment synopsis of your daily routine."

Sparing you the details of her trip to the toilet (I shit you not), she informed me that she had visited a record store, another store for some incense, a coffee shop that "was not Starbucks," a thrift store for some new clothes that were not new, and spent the day deciding where to place her new tattoo. She showed me a sketch of a circle with two parallel lines vertically going through it. Apparently it represents some reformed version of druidism. I'm not sure. She then confessed to not finishing a book review for one of her classes because, as she put it, "the real world has so much more to offer."

"Like buying stuff," I asked.

"What?"

"I mean, basically, it seems to me, and please correct me if I'm wrong, but you're just a typical college kid who doesn't do their work and really enjoys shopping. I don't see how your way of life is even remotely different from anyone else. If anything, it is the exact *opposite* of offering an alternative to what you referred to as 'Westernized' teachings. Your spiritualized anti-religious faith fits perfectly in the system. You make a wonderful capitalist, you just accessorize differently from the Christians."

She sat there with her eyes shut and a strange look on her face—like she was constipated (based on what she had previously told me, it was highly unlikely). She was kind of grimacing; it looked like she was trying to wish me off the planet. I couldn't tell if she was taking it in or if she was having an acid flashback. Either way, I genuinely wanted to help her be the kind of interesting person she was desperately trying so hard to be. I told her that my interest with her posse of neo-pagans was due to my hope that they were going to present an alternative to the nonsense currently consuming all of us. I suggested that we were all being duped into thinking there was some sort of out and expressed my concern that, contrary to her best intentions, she was actually being trained to be exactly what she was claiming she didn't want to be. She was being trained to fit within the system by purchasing her rebellion. This lovely, hairy druid was a picture-perfect example of what it means to be owned by a system that deceives us into thinking we can escape being owned. It is, forgive the pop culture reference, the matrix being the matrix. The matrix dupes us into thinking we can see our way out of the matrix by spiritualizing Eastern religions or—in her case, a religion from antiquity—as a possible way out. The fact that the matrix encourages us to do this, in order to escape it, is further proof that we are only falling deeper and deeper into the matrix precisely because we think we have somehow escaped it.

I love that film, even the third one.

She told me I was a very pessimistic person, that she would not stoop to my level of cynicism, and that I was being reductionistic.

"Name one thing," I challenged her, "that is not reducible to the market."

Warning: Make sure you do not have anything in your mouth when you are reading this, I would hate for it to come spewing out all over the pages of this lovely book.

Are you ready? Are you ready for the one thing she named that is not reducible to the market? Are you sure? Please, make sure you're ready. Okay, I think you're ready. Here is the one thing she told me is not reducible to the market.

"Love."

It would be impossible to tell you how long I laughed, or how many hours passed by as I rolled on the ground, tears flowing out of my eyes, as I thought about the millions of movies, magazines, books, comics, poems, songs, plays, television shows, commercials, advertisements, internet matchmaking Websites, *ad nauseum ad infinitum,* not to mention the second most important spending day of the year, Valentine's Day, before I almost passed out for lack of breathing.

This was one funny girl.

Watching me writhe in pain, I daresay it would be an understatement to suggest she was annoyed with me. She told me I needed to "stop looking for the bad in everything."

I asked her if wearing crystals would help me be more positive, and, if so, how much would they cost?

At this point, she told me our conversation was over because she didn't "need to be subjected to antagonistic people" like myself. I apologized for coming across as such a jerk, I just wanted to help her see that her claim to be "spiritual, not religious" simply meant she was owned by that religious institution known as capitalism, and that we are all just targets of marketing schemes designed to convince us to sacrifice at its chief temple—the mall. It's who owns us. We're all shoppers. We shop for mates, friends, clothes, food, entertainment, religions, as well as various forms of spirituality. Spirituality is a very conducive form of life to free-market capitalism because what it means to be spiritual is whatever you want it to mean—which means the market will dictate what you need to purchase in order to be authentic to your own inner self.

It's a vicious circle.

It does, however, have me thinking: if I were Satan, how would I best trick people into giving over their bodies for something that so succinctly takes on the vices of the seven deadly sins? What would I need to create in order to turn greed into a virtue? What would I need to invent that could bind together people of any nationality, creed, or faith in such a way that they could agree that such a thing was worth dying and killing for? What would I need to create that would be an unquestionable good that all of life can be reduced to? That is, what would I have to design in order to thoroughly own the human race?

And then, like a flash of lighting from the heavens, I saw Satan fall. I made my way over to investigate, and in the rubble I found a lone book. It was Adam Smith's *The Wealth of All Nations*.

SOME SATANIST YOU ARE,
YOU SOUND MORE LIKE A CHRISTIAN

The devil is a better theologian than any of us and is a devil still.
—A. W. Tozer

Hopefully, my transition from Satanism to Adam Smith is not met without at least some sense of humor (along with my slight modification to Luke 10:18). As intentional as it may be to position the writer of *The Wealth of Nations* between neo-druidism and Satanism, I am, of course, not suggesting Smith was either. Rather, I am suggesting that druids, Satanists, and Christians, for that matter, differ very little in how they respond to the economic system that runs the world. I'm no longer sure that there is enough difference between these groups, outside of clothing apparel, to suggest anything other than common ownership by this socio-economic politic. I'm no longer even sure that the "big" differences between these groups are really that big.

We'll see.

Likewise, the first thing I discovered in my conversations with Satanists is that they are a whole lot like Christians. By this, I mean many things. First of all, they are a highly schismatic bunch. Just as Christianity is divided into countless denominations (who cares that St. Paul claims unity to be the chief factor amongst Christians?), Satanists too are quite divided on what form proper worship requires. In some ways, this simply has more to do with the way Satanism has developed in the modern West. By modern, I am referring to the ideology known as modernity or classical liberalism. Satanists may trace their roots back to the first born creation of God, Lilith (Adam's supposed first wife), or any number of high-ranking Egyptian gods, but, just like all of us, they cannot deny being subject to the philosophical and cultural indoctrination that trains us to think of ourselves primarily in hyper-individualistic terms. Schisms are a philosophical necessity of our age. The divide between Satanists, however, takes two very strong forms: first, there are those Satanists who believe in the existence of Satan (theistic Satanists), and, second, there are those Satanists who do not believe in the existence of Satan.

I know. Strange, right?

Just like Christians, there are some who believe in Satan and some who do not; most Satanists scoff at the idea of an actual fallen angelic creature. In quite possibly the holiest of all texts for many Satanists, *The Satanic Bible*, Anton LaVey argues that most "Satanists do not accept Satan as an anthropomorphic being with cloven hooves, a barbed tail, and horns."[3] LaVey argues that such a notion is nothing more than a grandiose invention created by the religious hierarchy of various faith traditions in order to maintain some sort of order over humanity's natural desires. Satan, LaVey continues, is not a god, a demi-god, nor a fallen angel; Satan represents a force of nature that is natural to all humans that religions, Christianity in particular, have attempted to tame or domesticate for its own expansion.[4] LaVey came upon this notion while he was pulling double duty as an organist in carnivals and tent-show revivals. On Saturday nights, LaVey found many pious men, both young and old, lusting after the women dancing at the carnival. He would see these same men on Sunday mornings repenting to church leaders for acting on their sinful desires. Saturday night would roll back around, and present were the same men. Sunday morning proved to be a repetition of the previous Sunday. And so on and so on.

The church, argues LaVey, is doing great harm by attempting to repress what is nothing more than the natural desires of humans. Like any other animal, we are merely acting upon our biologically driven desires for self-fulfillment. This can take the shape of sex, greed, lust, or gluttony—all of which claims LaVey, are natural. These natural impulses are what make humans human, yet the church considers them to be a vice. In this regard, the church is the true adversary of humanity—Satan, if you will—as it attempts to suppress what is only natural to being human. To clarify exactly what Satanism represents, LaVey constructed "The Nine Satanic Statements." I cite them in their totality, with a bit of running commentary, for your own spiritual (or material, as the case may be) edification:

1. Satan represents indulgence, instead of abstinence! *(Save for a random few intentional communities, who in our culture, under this definition, is not a Satanist?)*

3. LaVey, *Satanic Bible*, 62.
4. Ibid., 62–63.

2. Satan represents vital existence, instead of spiritual pipe dreams! *(Are any of the "New Atheists" even remotely original in their protest?)*

3. Satan represents undefiled wisdom, instead of hypocritical self-deceit! *(What is the difference between defiled wisdom and undefiled wisdom? Wouldn't defiled wisdom be an oxymoron? If so, what meaning does the adjective "undefiled" add to the term wisdom that is not already present in the meaning of the word wisdom? And how can one deceive one's self? Who is the "I" deceiving the "I"? If I can deceive myself, who is the "I" separate from the self that is the object of my inadvertent deception? Someone, it appears, needs to read Wittgenstein.)*

4. Satan represents kindness to those who deserve it, instead of love wasted on ingrates! *(Can't stand those ingrates.)*

5. Satan represents vengeance, instead of turning the other cheek! *(What kind of Christianity has LaVey witnessed? There is hardly a Christian in the United States, or in the world for that matter—save for the Anabaptists and the thirty-two Catholic and Methodist pacifists I know—that does not favor any alternative to turning the other cheek.)*

6. Satan represents responsibility to the responsible instead of concern for psychic vampires! *(Is that like a telepathic Lestat or the spiritual guru/automaton Joel Osteen?)*

7. Satan represents man as just another animal, sometimes better, more often worse, than those that walk on all fours, who, because of his "divine spiritual and intellectual development," has become the most vicious animal of all! *(Okay, you got me. I actually agree with this one.)*

8. Satan represents all of the so-called sins, as they all lead to physical, mental, or emotional gratification! *(As well as obesity, health problems, STD's, capitalism, the free market, idolatrous allegiance to nation-states, and The Grammy's.)*

9. Satan has been the best friend the church has ever had, as he has kept it in business all these years! *(Does this mean that without the church there wouldn't be any Satanists, or Anton LaVey, Peter H. Gilmore, or the Sethian Liberation Front? Talk about being reactionary . . .)*

As I first examined these core principles I couldn't help but think, "Wow, he sure likes Ayn Rand."

He also appears to like exclamation points, but we won't hold that against him.

Basically, this credo is nothing more than modern political philosophy delivered by a guy with an insatiably narcissistic desire to be noticed (Look at my piercings! Look at my tattoos! Look at my scary goatee! Look at me! Look at me!) and a love for really, really bad music. Honestly, on this latter point, every person I could find—whether that was some sort of "High Priest" or "Priestess"[5] or some low-ranking pawn who practices their devotion to Satanism or The Temple of Set through the internet—loved some hybrid form of death metal/glam rock/indie-infused compost.

I engaged a number of Satanists of various stripes in conversation, but I could never get over how unabashedly similar to everyone else these people were. Like the aforementioned druid, the only real difference I could discern was their love for the color black.

Being a Mennonite, I'm okay with this color preference.

It doesn't seem to matter if the Satanist in question believes in the existence of Satan or denies the literal existence of Satan. Akin to the Unitarians, and most people of a modern persuasion, they are following their own pursuit of what makes them happy. As LaVey claims, a person should follow their own desires as far as they want up to the point that it brings another person harm—unless, that is, such a person wishes to be harmed. How is this any different from how Locke and Rousseau imagined modern politics? For that matter, how is this any different than the average Christian buying into the language and logic of modern politics latticed upon its grammatical framework of autonomy, rights, and the pursuit of happiness? Did modernity, while making belief in the Devil less credible, not, in turn, create a society in which the logical outcome is LaVey's understanding of Satanism? How is such a philosophy any different from how the average person lives her life? How is it any different from how the average *Christian* lives her life?

For instance, and in order to piggyback on LaVey's creed, in his book *The Black Arts*, Richard Cavendish argues, "The followers of the Devil are intensely excited by and preoccupied with sensual pleasure and worldly

---

5. For a group that hates religious hierarchies so much, they definitely do not mind forming their own.

achievement. They admire pride, strength, and force."[6] If you were to sub-
stitute "the Devil" with "Jesus in the United States" would there be any
denying that this is true? More than 75 percent of all people in the United
States claim to be Christian. Such people purport to follow a king who
said that his kingdom was not of this world. Yet, if such people follow a
person whose kingdom is not of this world, what are they doing propping
up an empire that has more than eight hundred military bases stationed
throughout the globe? You simply cannot get any more "worldly" than
that. This ever-expanding empire, made possible by the domination of
natural resources protected by the world's largest military, is the epitome
of "pride, strength, and force." When Cavendish claims that Satanists
admire these cardinal virtues of nationalism, I just have to wonder how
American Christians differ on the subject.

This is not the only place Cavendish seems to misinterpret the majority of Christianity's practitioners. He claims that worshippers of the
Devil consider the Christian practice of self-denial and humility to be
"spineless."

Again, what Christian has this person been observing?[7]

Self-denial is an absolute crime in our culture. If you start denying
yourself material goods you will end up destroying our very precarious
economy. It is an absolute moral obligation of all citizens, Christian or
not, to indulge their every whim, to buy the biggest house, to purchase
a new car every four years, to shop for new clothes, accessories, games,
etc., in short, to never be satisfied, to be perpetually in need of more, all
in order to perfect the capitalist virtue known as greed. How dare these
Satanists and black magicians accuse Christians of not fulfilling their
moral obligation to perpetuate the American Way of Life! We can be preoccupied with sensual pleasure, worldly achievement, pride, strength, and
force as much as anyone else! Indeed, I think we are close to perfecting it.
Have the Satanists not paid any attention to the ease by which Christians
participate in war? The obvious contradiction of Christians killing their
enemies in the name of the God who tells them to love their enemies
does not cause even the slightest feeling of discomfort for the majority
of North American Christians. Have these Satanists ever stepped foot in
a Christian Family Bookstore and counted the number of books glorify-

6. Cavendish, *Black Arts*, 290.

7. Okay, in an effort to be charitable, perhaps he knows about Dorothy Day or Thomas
Merton. It's a long shot, but I'm willing to give him the benefit of the doubt.

ing war in their Christian Inspiration section? Next to books about so-called radical discipleship one will find such Christ-inspired literature as *Lessons on the Battlefield*, *The Patriot's Bible*, and Walker, Texas Ranger's soon to be classic, *Blackbelt Patriotism*—because, you know, Jesus was so obviously a fan of both the state (killed by it) and karate (taught nonviolence). In case reading is not your thing, there are also miniature solid gold crosses, encrusted with diamonds and draped with American flags, available for purchase for those needing to prove their faith and pride in a tribal god that has far more in common with Ares, the god of war, than Jesus, the Prince of Peace.

Silly Satanists.

We are far better at worshipping your god than you will ever be.

5 Finding, Binding, and "Get Behind Me" Satan

But who prays for Satan? Who, in eighteen centuries, has had the common humanity to pray for the one sinner that needed it most?

—Mark Twain

I have dealt with demons of all sorts of illnesses and addictions, from cerebral palsy to schizophrenia and from heroin addiction to compulsive masturbation.

—Bob Larson

As my subjects in chapter 4 suggested, we are dealing with an impulse, a spirit, so to speak, not a genuine being. Their denial of a literal Satan, replaced by this more spiritual omnipresence, is not a far cry from St. Paul's proclamation that our struggle is not against flesh and blood, but "against the spiritual forces of evil in the heavenly places" (Eph 6:12). Nevertheless, many Christians (and non-Christians) refuse to simply spiritualize the issue. They contend that the Devil and his minions are material beings bent on nothing more than the annihilation of creation. Many people claim to have seen these beings, been haunted by them, possessed by them, and some have even had sex with them.

"How did that work out for you?" I asked the admittedly willing participant of an ongoing incubus-based relationship.

"I've had worse," she told me. "I'm not much into cuddling, so it's great that he's gone by the time I wake up."

"Wow," I said. "You're every man's dream."

"Maybe so," she admitted. "But unfortunately for you human boys I'm happily monogamous."

I don't think it's possible to get much more monogamous than a relationship that only occurs in your dreams. And I should know.

While it was certainly not a problem locating people claiming first-hand experience with Satan and/or demons, trying to locate a person who would allow me an "in" on such an experience was next to impossible. I contacted countless people and groups who claimed to specialize in everything from demon conjuration to spiritual warfare asking them if they would allow me to tag along.

Repeatedly I was told, "It's too dangerous." In the case of the spiritual warriors I contacted, I was informed that it was simply too risky to be around an authentic exorcism. Despite the fact that I have spent my entire life in the church, as well as a dozen years obtaining a bachelors, masters, and a doctoral degree in theology, all from Christian schools, I was still not capable of being able to handle a real experience with a demon—much less their boss. I was given an entire litany of reasons as to why I was not allowed to accompany spiritual warriors on their battles: I'm an academic; I'm a casual observer; I'm not "right" with God; I do not have a sufficient enough prayer life; I have never been slain in the spirit, experienced holy laughter, or spoken in tongues.

What makes Pentecostals, fundamentalists, and non-academics so demon impervious?

One non-Pentecostal spiritual warrior I spoke with, who traveled with a team out of Nashville, Tennessee, informed me that demons, once exorcised, immediately look for a host who is susceptible to possession (as previously discussed in chapter 3). Assuming he was suggesting I would be the likely candidate for possession, I quickly inserted, "That's what I'm hoping for, that's the whole point!" Before he could hang up the phone, I told him if they are such powerful spiritual warriors surely it would not be a problem to exorcise the demon from me.

"You have no idea," he informed me, "what that experience could do to you."

"No, you're right, but it sure would help book sales."

He wasn't swayed, so I reminded him that whenever Jesus healed a demoniac they seemed to recover perfectly well. Once the demon or demons were gone, they appeared to be gone forever. It's sort of like getting chickenpox: once you have them you can't get them again.

I'm trying to think of this as a vaccination.

It seems relatively safer this way, too. If I'm ever going to risk demonic possession I want it to be in the company of some righteous warriors so they can get it out of me. Smart, right?

Alas, no one would take me up on my experiment. Despite the fact that the Devil is roaming the world looking for souls to steal (thank you Charlie Daniels), there do not appear to be any Christians willing to help me prove his existence. I decided to take a different approach, a more direct one. Due to the number of people warning me about the occult, I can only assume it is within their domain that I will locate the Prince of Darkness. I want to make sure I get this right so I return to a number of authors and speakers who remain highly influential in matters of spiritual warfare. I seek their authoritative expertise because, as one spiritual warrior informed me, "When it comes to the Devil, there's no room for error."

NOW YOU SATAN, NOW YOU DON'T: MEET BOB "I EXORCISED DEATH" LARSON

Unfortunately, long distance exorcisms can give Satan the upper hand. The unclean spirit can manifest and use the victim's body to make him hang up the phone.

—Bob Larson

A return trip to the local Christian Family Bookstore proved quite helpful. There is certainly no shortage of resources for those interested in either material or spiritual warfare. I picked up a number of books that purported to be highly influential for people engaged in the subject of spiritual warfare. I examined such gems as Doris Wagner's *How to Cast out Demons*, Neil Anderson's *Victory Over the Darkness*, and Bob Larson's *Larson's Book of Spiritual Warfare*.

You have to admire any author conceited enough to name a book after himself.

Bob Larson is, or at least claims to be, a greatly respected, admired, and authoritative source on all things evil. Even the demons are impressed by his renowned wisdom on spiritual warfare. He claims a demon once asked him how he knew all the rules and regulations for spiritual warfare.

"Someone from our side must have taught you," the demon told Larson. "I have never met anyone who knows the rules as well you do."[1]

High praise, coming from a demon.

I guess Larson would have to be "the man" when it comes to exorcisms as he claims to have faced, and defeated, not only the Egyptian sun-god Ra, but the actual rider on the pale horse in Revelation 6—Death.

Now *that* is a resumé.

At one time, he was a radio personality and traveled extensively not only to lecture on spiritual warfare but to exorcise demons (and gods). His book was so utterly fascinating, as he promised it would be in the introduction, that I read all four hundred plus pages over a two-day time period. The book is something of an autobiography detailing his countless exorcisms and the many things he has learned about the occult. *Larson's Book of Spiritual Warfare* claims to provide the reader with the tools necessary to locate demons, to find out what attracts them, and how to, ultimately, exorcise them.

Sounds like the perfect book for my project.

He also provides a wealth of information on worldly philosophies that fall under the domain of the occult. I found this part to be exceptionally helpful as there were many things I was surprised to discover were demonic. Below is a short list of occult-based practices and ideologies, according to Bob "Exorcist of Death" Larson, that could result in your being possessed by a demon:

- feminism
- nuclear disarmament
- organic foods
- minority rights
- the sharing of natural resources

This is not all of course. He also lists role-playing games, T'ai Chi, The Rocky Horror Picture Show, herbs, "daddy issues," homosexuality, dressing in black, reflexology, and compulsive masturbation.

I'm not touching that one.

---

1. Larson, *Larson's Book of Spiritual Warfare*, 435.

But it is the five listed above I find to be the most interesting, as I was under the impression that things like healthy food and the rights of women and minorities were good things. Apparently, the Devil has pulled a quick one on me. As best as I can discern, I offer you my humble understanding as to why Larson finds the above list demonic:

1. Feminism—Feminism is a source of evil because it implants in women the idea that they are human beings.

2. Nuclear Disarmament—Activists who desire the elimination of nuclear weapons do not understand that we have to destroy the earth before we get a better one.

3. Organic Foods—It is good to eat processed foods splattered with pesticides and injected with hormones. Only someone involved with the occult would ever be concerned with the packaging of food and the overall desire to know what is going into one's body. The adage "you are what you eat," Larson argues, "literally guides the occult approach to cooking."[2]

4. Minority Rights—Becky Fischer, children's pastor of *Jesus Camp*, appears to agree with Larson when she says, "The problem with democracy is that it has to give everyone equal rights." As Christians, we should be opposed to anything that may be fair for all people. This is a wonderful witnessing tool, along with our Jesus fashion wear, as it will make non-Christians want to become Christians so they can have rights, too.

5. Sharing of Natural Resources—Those engaged in the occult, so claims Larson, have the preposterous idea that the natural resources of the earth should belong to everyone. Silly demon-possessed people, don't you understand that resources should only belong to the people rich and powerful enough to obtain it? If we give poor people things like food and shelter, what will happen to the incentive to better one's self? As Larson claims, the duty of the Christian is to generate wealth, not to share it. (Of course, he has to overlook the more than 1,500 references in the Bible that are opposed to this notion, but, hey, he took out Death, what do I know?)[3]

After enlightening us with some of the tactics of the Devil—how he tempts us to believe in things like equality, healthy food, and peace—

2. Ibid., 234.

3. Ibid., 233–39, 293–300

Larson buttresses his case by telling stories of one-on-one confrontations with demonically possessed people. I find this part to be especially compelling because Larson is kind enough to always explain how these people came under the influence of Satan. This intrigues me, of course, because if this is true it should prove very beneficial to my research.

For instance, and to build upon the above list, Larson claims that many of the demons he exorcised gained power over people through the bold and insidious channels of darkness like *Advanced Dungeons and Dragons,* films such as *Halloween* and *Friday the 13th,* and television shows like *Sabrina the Teenage Witch.*

Oh, Melissa Joan Hart. You do inspire in me naughty thoughts.

However, one need not engage in the watching of such horror films or bad television shows to become a slave to Satan. For instance, Larson describes one young boy, Randy, who was violently possessed by a demon named "Pride" because Randy enjoyed driving a car.[4]

Before moving on, I should point out that the demons in Larson's book have incredibly lackluster names. Their names, or perhaps I should call them titles, include: Pride, Destruction, Disobedience, Envy, Alcohol, Anger, and one girl whose demons were named—and brace yourself for this because I am not making this up—Double D.

That's a demon I wouldn't mind getting in touch with sometime.

Anyway, they had problems exorcizing Randy's demon because Randy was too attached to his vehicle. Being the child of impoverished farmers, the only thing that enabled Randy to feel better about himself was the car he had worked so hard to purchase. Larson told him that if he wanted to be free of his demons he would have to sell his car and give all the money to the church. Randy initially resisted (and who wouldn't?), but eventually the rather impoverished youth submitted to the spiritual authority of Larson, sold his car, and gave the money to the church.

Now I ask you, who was really screwing Randy? The demons or the exorcist?

After reading about half of Larson's book, I came to the realization that I may have just found Satan. Why he would choose to go by the name "Bob" is a mystery to me. He should have chosen "Richard."

How wonderfully clever, though, of Satan to write a book about how to expose and defeat Satan, that would in actuality continue to under-

4. Ibid., 307–15.

write his reign. That is just brilliant. The more I think about it, the more sense it makes. If you were Satan wouldn't you write a book about how to triumph over evil that provides all the wrong advice on how to triumph over evil? By pretending to be an exorcist, Satan convinces his readers to neglect healthy food, promote nuclear weapons, re-establish sexist and racist laws, exploit natural resources, and avoid stretching exercises.

That's just crafty.

Really, really crafty.

Problem is, now I'm no longer sure what I need to do to warrant Satan's attention. I drink organic milk, I think nuclear weapons are the scourge of the earth, I stand in a rich Christian tradition that claims goods are only good if they are shared, and I occasionally wear black (I am, after all, a Mennonite). Does this mean, at least according to the criteria Larson sketches, my body is a container of demons? I have not exhibited any thrashing around. I have yet to levitate or become catatonic while voices who sound like their author is a bad fiction writer claim ownership of my body. What's going on? I, along with countless friends, many of whom are theologians and pastors, perfectly embody Larson's criteria. Why are we not yet possessed? Maybe, and I can only speak for myself, I'm just not intense enough in my pursuit. Perhaps I should be experimenting with the more traditional occult practices.

To his credit, Larson does point out the staples of the occult community: tarot cards, astrology, runes, and magic. He has a plethora of biblical references to warn people to avoid the power latent within these practices. The Bible, in its condemnation of certain practices affiliated with the occult, never denies its power. On the contrary, it suggests there is something dangerous behind these practices—therein offering evidence that there is a dark reality beyond the material for me to discover. The Bible does not suggest that astrology, sorcery, speaking with spirits, or anything of that nature is phony, it simply instructs us not to participate in them.

> When you come into the land that the Lord your God is giving you, you must not learn to imitate the abhorrent practices of those nations. No one shall be found among you who makes a son or daughter pass through fire, or who practices divination, or is a soothsayer, or an augur, or a sorcerer, or one who casts spells, or who consults ghosts or spirits, or who seeks oracles from the dead. For whoever does these things is abhorrent to the Lord . . .
> (Deut 18:9–12a).

That pretty much eliminates all of my best options.

This is not the only passage wherein God reveals God's repugnance for what is commonly referred to as the occult. Although the word "occult" simply refers to something that is hidden—as in hidden knowledge[5]—it now bears the connotations of those people who practice these very things forbidden by God. Unfortunately, if I'm ever going to locate Satan, these now seem like my best options. After all, it only makes sense that Satan would be behind those things God considers wicked.

I am, it appears, in quite the conundrum.

I wish to avoid the fate of Queen Jezebel who practiced sorcery and was punished by being thrown out of a window. The second book of Kings claims that "her blood splattered on the wall and on the horses, which trampled her." When a few eunuchs attempted to bury her, the only thing they found were her "skull and the feet and the palms of her hands." Dogs consumed her flesh and her corpse became dung on a field (2 Kgs 9:33–37).

I do not want to end up as dung on a field.[6]

Given that Lev 20:27 demands the stoning of anyone who is a medium or a wizard, and Revelation 8 claims that sorcerers will find themselves in "the lake that burns with fire and sulfur," I think I will pass on becoming the next Harry Potter. I have retained too much fear of God (as well as a familiarity with numerous passages where God has killed people over a whole lot less—poor Onan) to approach what follows without some serious fear and trembling. But approach it, I must.

THELEMA AND LOUISE;
OR, HOLY SMOKE BAPHOMET!

The clever see danger and hide; but the simple go on, and suffer for it.

—Proverbs 27:12

---

5. And, once again, we're back to Gnosticism.

6. This is not the only warning given to those who engage in fortune-telling, channeling, or divination. Other passages that forbid God's people from engaging in such activities include: Isa 8:19, 19:3, 44:25; Jer 14:14, 29:9; 2 Kgs 21:6, 23:24; Ezek 21:21; 1 Sam 28; and 1 Chron 10:13–14.

Finding a practicing pagan, a theistic Satanist, or a practitioner of white or black magic (if there really is a distinction) who was genuinely open for a conversation that could be used in this book was trickier than I thought. Every person I talked to was incredibly reluctant to give too much away. They wanted you to submit to their discipline, invest your life in their rituals and practices, and only then could you learn their trade secrets. There would be no information without some sort of ascetic sacrifice.

Fair enough. I respect that. It just makes it difficult to learn anything as an outsider.

"How would you like to be a Mennonite for a few months?" I asked one guy who claimed to be a sorcerer.

"I don't think I would," he said. "I'll take my car over your buggy. Though that is pretty cool about the whole multiple wives thing."

I let him know we didn't all drive buggies, nor were we from Utah. I also told him if he didn't submit to our way of life I wasn't going to let him in on any of our big, hidden, underground, archaic secrets.

"You guys don't have any secrets . . . do you?"

I offered to become a sorcerer for a month if he would become a Mennonite for a month. I think that would make for an interesting television show. Instead of spouse swapping, one would swap religious identities. The prize would be an eternity in heaven, hell, or nirvana, but you would have to wait until the season after the last season to find out whether or not you won.

Yes, that was a Kafka reference.

After numerous dead-ends, I was in a small town in Kentucky when my luck changed. As fortune would have it, I ran into a shamanistic healer quite willing to share his occultist life experiences with me.

Meeting at a small Greek diner, my new friend and I broke bread and discussed the finer points of paganism, necromancy, witchcraft, and how to conjure spirits. All that was required on my part was a willingness to listen and the promise that I would not share his name. In fact, he refused to give me his or his friends magical names as they "are so well known, people in my community would know exactly who I am talking about."

The first question I had for him revolved around his "body art." He was covered with tattoos including Hebrew, a pentagram, references to Norse deities, as well Siddhartha Gautama sitting under the Bodhi tree.

This guy was a walking world religions course.

"What's the deal with the Buddha tattoo?" I asked.

"It serves to remind me to not act under selfish desires."

"Nothing wrong with that," I said.

I asked him about who he was, what religious backgrounds had shaped him, and what his position was in his specific faith community.

"Well," he told me, "I grew up interested in occult studies, from there I studied astrology—"

"Did you do much with tarot cards?"

"Yeah."

I was very interested in his response because the few fortune-tellers and palm readers I visited bored me. Like most astrologers, televangelists, and people such as Bill Maher, Glenn Beck, and Richard Dawkins, they're just in it for the money.

"Dude, straight up, be honest," I was a bit excited. "Did you find any validity in tarot cards? You know, some people are just out there making money by telling people a good fortune."

"Absolutely."

"But yet," I asked, "you would contend that there is still validity to such practices?"

"Oh yes. The times I found where it was most valid were more like prophecies coming true, or where the individual was able to take on this spirit. They were able to let go of their self and their own individual self to allow these things to flow through them or work through them. When doing the reading these things would manifest through them, so it wasn't as much as how they were interpreting them as much as how the spirit was interpreting this and they [tarot card readers] were used as a conduit. They were a sacred kind of conduit that allowed their energy to flow through them in order to communicate what was seen. You know, time is not this linear thing we like to think of as much as it is occurring all at once. If you were to draw a dot, behind that dot there would be infinite dots which is a timeline of time as we think, but that dot is still on top of every other dot that exists, making time simultaneous, and therefore easily understood in terms of the future. But the future is not really the future, in essence, and that is why we, and tarot card readers, can see it."

I really dig that "non-linear nature of time" stuff. That's how, by the way, comic book writers are often able to resurrect their fallen heroes. Eternal recurrence meet Steve Rogers and Bruce Wayne.

"Gotcha. Okay, going back . . . when you say the occult, is this the dark arts or what you would call black magic?"

"Yeah, but there are a lot of different things at work," he explained. "I lived in this one house, we were a family of sorts, about fifteen of us. And we all had our strong points, and we would practice those and put more emphasis on those points, and then we would allow those, each with their own strong points, to take care of certain things that one of us on our own couldn't deal with. We were an occult family. Some of my friends were really good at drawing in spirits."

I asked him what he meant by drawing in spirits.

"It's almost like an invocation. Calling spirits to enter you and to speak through you to the point that you are no longer talking to the individual, you are talking to whatever spirit has entered them."

"How does this happen?" I asked. "Do you have to conjure specific spirits, or is it a general conjuration? Does it have anything to do with where you live?"

"That's a good question," he told me. "We would generally pick houses that we knew had a lot of energy working through them, and eventually you learn how to open up certain frequencies that allow spirits to move through them."

"So," I asked, "it's not so much that you command or you force a spirit to do your bidding, you know, some kind of slave spirit working for the one who mastered some spell, rather, you throw out some frequency that allows them to choose to enter, or is there a way to sort of force their hand?"

"Yeah, yeah, you can do that."

"Does that piss them off?" I asked.

"Yeah, it depends. You know, like necromancers, and I didn't know very many of them, but in essence when you study necromancy it is all about the ability to have these spirits conform to your will. They pretty much do whatever you want them to do because, if not, they are going to suffer whatever consequences you think are necessary."

"Well, what is that like?" I asked. "If you are already in the spirit world or whatever, what are bad consequences for a spirit?"

"Just like there are different realms there are different layers of reality. From the physical all the way up to spiritual, as well as astro-realms. You could trap them in a realm that was not to their liking, or, you could bind them with another energy that is very uncomfortable. You could also trap them inside of an object, and then just bring them out whenever you felt like using them and then put them away."

"Are there any examples of the spirits retaliating in any way?" I asked.

"Oh yeah. Absolutely. That is actually quite popular."

"Retaliation?"

"Yeah, absolutely."

"So, you have to be pretty good at what you are doing in the sense of exercising some sort of control over these spirits?" I asked.

"Yeah, and that takes time and a certain amount of personal power, and it still backfires sometimes."

"Do you have any kind of examples?"

"Yeah, yeah," he said. "I was living in this house and essentially some of the guys living there thought it was going to be a great idea to bind these spirits in this book and put it in the basement. And they did that, and they performed a binding ritual, and they took the spirits and put them in the book."

I asked him if knew the title of the book. When he told me he couldn't remember, I asked him if it was Niebuhr's *Christ and Culture*.

"I don't know," he responded. "I don't think so. Why?"

"Well, if I was going to bind a spirit to a book, especially if it was a demon, it would be that one. That book is terrible. Absolutely terrible. If I could bind a demon to any one book it would be that one. Well, either that or Fletcher's *Situation Ethics*."

"Yeah, I don't know those—"

"Or, Heidegger's *Being and Time*. Do you know Heidegger? No? He was a Nazi."

He nodded his head letting me know he would stay clear of these books. Then he continued, "Now, when that happened, when they bound the spirit to the book, I don't believe that spell was powerful enough to bind those particular spirits because I almost think in essence there was energy there, some random spirits, some of them that were probably human at one time and then some that weren't. They were like, and I'm not saying they were a whole deity, or an entire deity was trapped in that house, I'm saying there was a piece of that deity's energy that was trapped in that time-space. And so it retaliated and it broke the binding like it was nothing, like it was a piece of silly string or something. What happened then was a retaliation of sorts which was really like, you know, lessons to be learned—about what is okay and what is not okay. It's like it is saying, 'How dare you try to bind me, something that is eternal, something that is bigger than the world you live in, something that is more powerful than you can ever possibly imagine. How dare you try to bind me with mere words.' You know, it was such disrespect for something that powerful."

I asked him how the spirit responded to their disrespect.

"Well, prior to this, we never had any sort of bug or cockroach problem. The following day, after all of this, I would say that there were hundred of thousands of bugs everywhere in our house. They were even trapped in our ear canals. We woke up with them in our ears; you could feel them trying to burrow deeper in our ear canals."

That's nasty.

I asked what the next step is after spirit retaliation. For instance, do you have to call Orkin? If so, I hypothesized, could it be possible that the spirit is in cahoots with bug exterminators and that, maybe, the whole thing is just a big racket?

This guy was pretty awesome because rather than get annoyed with me, he just laughed at my juvenile sarcasm. He told me there was no exterminator capable of taking care of this bug problem. Instead, you have to appease the angered spirit.

Before doing this, however, he explained to me how they tried trapping it again, this time using symbols and a Golem. He told me they used a mannequin in order to try to trap the spirit.

I knew there was a legitimate reason for my fear and loathing of puppets—from which mannequins are an obvious species.

"Why a mannequin?" I asked.

"Because they look human, yet there is no spirit inside. You need an empty vessel. You could even use a dead cat."

"Wait, so a mannequin or a dead cat will work?"

"Sure, yeah," he responded. "Or a dead dog or any empty vessel will work."

"Do these empty vessels dupe them somehow?"

"No, these runes just attract them," he told me. "It attracts their frequency. It is almost like this mathematical equation for putting this thing here."

At this point in the conversation, he started to withhold certain information. The more I pushed him on specifics, the more reticent he became in giving precise details on how to conjure, trap, and bind spirits. He told me it was far too dangerous to speak of this so carelessly, lest the information were to fall in the wrong hands, or, simply put, inexperienced hands.

He did tell me that their second attempt to bind/trap this spirit went awry as well. He said that in their dreams, this mannequin would come to life and cause certain physical problems on each of those living in the house that would manifest themselves in the waking world. Their health and their ability to make money immediately declined.

I asked him how they addressed the situation, and he told me that due to his study of Rakhi and shamanistic healing, he started allowing such energy to serve as treatment on people who required it. This made him more and more powerful, and, along with his wife who was his apprentice in this form of healing, they were able to mend the riff between this energy and theirs that was causing so many problems.

"We cursed ourselves," he told me. "So, we had to find a way to undo the curse."

We continued talking about a large number of things found in witchcraft, the occult and even other religions. We talked about astral projection via yoga, traveling through the spirit world through shamanistic drumming and sweat teepees, as well as those people who attempt to conjure demons for whatever purpose they have in mind.

"What do you think," I asked him "about the kind of person who attempts to conjure, contact, or find some proof of demons, or even the Devil, if it is for the purpose of the academy, or even the existence of God?"

I explained to him about my student's search for the Devil as an attempt to prove the existence of God. I told him that despite how tongue and cheek I may seem in my line of questioning, I intend to be more than a casual traveler through his world. I am genuinely looking for something substantial.

"So," I told him, "I'm asking you right now to set me up with somebody who is going to make me either see this reality, or just feel it in a way that I know, in the most profound sense of the word 'know,' that it exists. Make it happen for me so that I have something to record in this book."

He asked me if it has to be the "main one," or if I would be willing to settle for lesser demons.

"At this point," I said, "I'll take what I can get."

He thought about it for a second or two then apologetically offered, "I could tell you that I could probably make that happen . . . but will I? Absolutely not."

"Aw, come on," I pleaded. "Why not?"

He explained that one reason it would be difficult is because he questioned the sincerity of my belief in the things he was telling me.

"You have to have reverence for these things," he said.

Which I find to be an interesting choice of words as reverence is very similar to the word fear. People of the monotheistic religions are to practice reverence/fear of God; whether or not such reverence or fear should be extended to God's creation, even demons, is debatable.

He explained that despite my lip service to the possibility of their existence, without a deep down genuine belief in such entities, such demons would not be interested in proving their existence to me.

"I know, I get that," I admitted to him. "But I'm in need of something here, and perhaps, nothing will happen, and then again, perhaps something does happen and it messes me up, but this could prove to be a monumental moment for my research."

He refused to relent. Just like the Christian spiritual-warfare warriors, he explained to me that it is just not worth the risk. In his early twenties, due to the contact he made with such entities—the very ones I am trying to locate—he suffered numerous nervous breakdowns, lived in a mental institution for years, and still draws disability checks for his problems.

I wanted to ask him how the government or private insurers cover issues in which an illness is due to one messing with demons. I wonder if this will be covered under the new health care reform platform. If that is the case, it would seem that if you practice the dark arts, you should have higher premiums than those who do not.

I did ask him if he really thought all of these issues came from his contact with such entities.

"Absolutely," he said. "There is an absolute connection between the two. I was perfectly fine before delving into all of this stuff, and it almost killed me. And once you make contact, it will change you for life."

For this very reason, he refused to aid me in my quest for either the Devil or lesser demons. I am not even sure he even believed in the Devil. He told me that at one point in his life he was a "true Satanist," which is, according to him, a person who does not believe in the existence of Satan. To be a Satanist is to be your own god.

Sort of like a Unitarian . . . or a neo-druid . . . or an ethicist—you get the point.

He was, however, convinced that dark spirits, or what Christians would refer to as demons, do exist. Instead of offering me one-on-one contact with such entities, he kindly offered me the services of his shamanistic healing.

Best deal yet.

Even after explaining to me what shamanistic healing entails, I remain unsure of exactly what it is—other than it sounds oddly similar to chiropractics.[7]

I ended our discussion with one last question, "Do you think that through the conjuring of spirits or through some sort of pact, if I were to commit myself, I could make my loans disappear?"

He didn't even hesitate. He immediately responded, "Oh, yes. They would be gone."

"Really?" I ecstatically belted.

"Absolutely. I have no doubt that could happen."

"Well, you see, now you got me," I told him. "Because, they are burdensome, man. They're huge. They're huge."

"I know, I know." I love his sense of solidarity. "But what I have learned through this whole phase of my life, and the one major conclusion out of all of these experiences that I can draw, is that although your loans seems uncomfortable to you, and I know this will sound crazy, but greater things are going to come out of experiencing what you need to experience in order to pay them off."

I stared in utter disbelief. Of all the things he had told me, this was by far the least credible. "Yes," I said to him, as I nodded my head in agreement, "you are correct—that sounds crazy."

He laughed and proceeded to tell me I'll be a completely different person than what I would be if I didn't have to pay my loans.

I agreed.

I would be a person with money.

I can't believe it was my conversation with the one-time Satanist turned pagan/shamanistic-healer/drum-playing mystic who would be the one to teach me about character building.

Well, that interview was a bust.

---

7. Take that to mean whatever you want it to mean.

Some demons are just picky about these kinds of things. I get it though; I'm pretty OCD myself.

Oftentimes some sort of chanting must occur. Demons seem to be very fussy about the number of times you say the same thing. They're not interested in responding unless you hit a certain magical number of requests. They want to make sure you're very serious.

Next, you need to fill a jar or pouch with dirt from a cemetery, or some sort of relic from someone or something (depending on the particularities of the impending contract) to bring with you to the non-paved crossroads. What happens next is dependent upon what you want. Most of the conjurations and pacts I discovered were for people looking for fame, wealth, power, or some special talent. For instance, in the case of Robert Johnson, or perhaps even the great Italian violinist Niccolo Paganini, you may need to bring a guitar or violin with you in order to gain mastery over the instrument. For some practitioners of hoodoo, or the so-called black arts (as many magicians decry such a distinction between white and black magic), it may not even be necessary to sell your soul for this skill. Rather, you may just need to pay the piper a small fee. A silver coin perhaps.

Why the Devil needs money, I have no idea. I'm just telling you what I've learned.

I decided to do it. This clearly serves a purpose beyond me; this is for the general edification of all those still reading this book. I wasn't entirely convinced I would do it correctly, but I kept telling myself it can't be that hard. I mean, since the entire nation of Haiti, according to Pat Robertson, was capable of pulling it off, it can't be that difficult. He runs the 700 Club, so he has to be right.

An aside, but this is an important one: the fact that Robertson didn't break out with little holes all over his body after his "Haiti made a pact with Satan" comment is more than enough evidence that Voo Doo is bogus. Seriously, if that comment didn't warrant a "let's make a doll and poke it" reprisal from Voo Doo practitioners, then what does it take? In case any of you have forgotten his commentary on the tragedy that struck Haiti, here you go:

> Something happened a long time ago in Haiti, and people might
> not want to talk about it. They were under the heel of the French.
> You know, Napoleon III, or whatever. And they got together and
> swore a pact to the Devil. They said, "We will serve you if you'll

get us free from the French." True story. And so, the Devil said,
"Okay, it's a deal." . . . [E]ver since, they have been cursed by one
thing after another.[9]

Poor silly Haitians, you should have stuck with the French.

I like how Robertson knows exactly what the entire nation of Haiti
said to the Devil. I really enjoy how he refers to the French leader as
"Napoleon III, or whatever." But my favorite part in the entire bit is when
he says, "True story." You know, just in case anybody thought he was making it up.

Back to my pact with Satan.

I took a receipt of the very minimum amount of student loans I have
paid (interest rates are demonic) and placed it in a small bag meant to
hold gaming dice. Given what the Nazarene church teaches in regards to
role-playing games, I thought it was a nice touch. You know, just in case
the Nazarenes were right.

I decided to make Friday nights the night of my experiment.
Technically speaking, it was really Saturday morning as I was staying close
to the midnight hour. I chose Saturday over Sunday because that was the
original day of rest, and I figured that I should start the Sabbath off right.
If the Sabbath really is the day of rest, and the Devil loves idle hands, this
could explain his late Friday night/early Saturday morning shenanigans.
Plus, I assumed Satan was prepping to wreak havoc on sound equipment
on Sunday mornings, so he was probably in no mood to be bothered on
Saturday nights.

Ideally I would have traveled to Clarksdale, Mississippi, as I am all
about tradition, but it appears to have become a little tourist trap. I believe
Satan's work, at least at that historic location, is done. Anytime you can
capitalize off the possibility of someone selling his or her soul to Satan,
Satan has to feel a sense of pride. Anyway, I was hoping that one dirt
crossroads would be just as good as the next.

Once I located the ideal place for my experiment, just some back-
roads off Highway 62 in the lovely state of North Carolina, I contemplated
what I needed to take with me. I planned on being there for quite awhile,
so I took a number of books to make sure I was doing it correctly, as
well as provide some background reading to help prepare me for what I
was about to experience. The backpack I was sporting contained a wide

9. See the video online: http://www.youtube.com/watch?v=MOQrcg9y1iA.

array of books including Richard Cavendish's *The Black Arts* and Robert Masello's *Fallen Angels . . . and Spirits of the Dark.* Despite the latter sounding like a romance novel, it, unfortunately, was not. I also brought with me a Bible, as I wanted to ask Satan for his take on the "you can have all of the kingdoms of this world" temptation story. Finally, I brought with me a copy of Dante's *Inferno*, Milton's *Paradise Lost* (again, I'm interested in his opinion as to their authenticity), as well as a copy of Noam Chomsky's *Keeping the Rabble in Line.*

That had nothing to do with the task at hand; I just almost always have a Chomsky book with me.

I also brought some salt, as it seems to work wonders for the Winchester boys. Plus, legend has it that if you toss it over your left shoulder you can ward off the Devil—just in case this turns out to be a really bad idea. I brought some cards and dice as these things were once understood to be popular tools of the Devil. I sported a shoddy silver necklace as I haven't forgotten Mrs. Jacobs' words of wisdom on jewelry. Finally, I brought along a camera in hopes that we could take a picture together. Can you imagine that on my Facebook profile?

For an additional safety measure, I sketched out in the dirt (I can see why asphalt would have been a problem) a devil's trap for him and a circle for me.

Again, you know, just in case.

Since my grandmother used to warn me about the evils of alcohol I grabbed a bottle of Jack Daniels and some red wine.

In vino veritas.

I also brought my iPod along and very strategically picked out the right atmospheric music. As anyone who knows me well will tell you, I am obsessively neurotic about the kind of music played for certain occasions. Whether it is pre-show music in the theatre or just something to skateboard to, music means everything. It only seemed appropriate, therefore, to spend a significant amount of time agonizing over what I would listen to while awaiting the presence of Satan. I finally decided on three different playlists, as I didn't find it necessary to limit it to just one. Each playlist contained eighteen songs.

Yes, I was being symbolic.

For starters, I brought along music I've been told is particularly close to the heart and ears of Satan—especially, but not limited to, music in the

80s and 90s: Slayer, Iron Maiden, Samhain, Black Sabbath, and AC/DC. I would have included Marilyn Manson but his stuff is just plain silly.

In an effort to add to the rich symbolism, I will list, as a musical tutorial, the first six songs of each playlist.

1. AC/DC—"Highway to Hell"
2. The Misfits—"American Nightmare"
3. Motley Crue—"Shout at the Devil"
4. Danzig—"Twist of Cain"
5. INXS—"Devil Inside"
6. Queen—"Don't Stop Me Now"

I named that mix, *Hells Bells: Pat Robertson Hearts Freddie Mercury*.

Playlist number two included all of the appropriate old-school bluegrass gospel (and a few non-gospel) songs I could find. You know the film *O' Brother Where Art Thou*? That's my family. For my parents, grandparents, and great-grandparents, Christianity was a matter of "getting saved" with the help of music such as "Blessed Assurance," "Will the Circle Be Unbroken," "That Old Rugged Cross," and "I'll Fly Away." The latter song being, I contend, the quintessential Fred Sanford "I'm coming to join ya Elizabeth!" song. As fortune would have it, such music has had, for me anyway, the opposite effect as intended. For some reason, whenever I hear these songs I want to slam lots of whisky. Every time we would sing them, whether it was at church, a birthday party, a softball game, a wedding, a funeral, or a bar mitzvah (seriously, had we ever been invited to a bar or bat mitzvah my family would have requested such songs), it made me want to get drunk.

Go figure.

Due to the nature of my fascination with the amalgamation of alcohol and gospel music, I decided it only fitting to include some less orthodox versions of the above genre. Here are the first six songs on playlist number two, appropriately titled, *The Devil Says I'm Out, but The Lord Says I'm Safe (Ode to Billy Sunday)*:

1. Jerry Lee Lewis—"The Old Rugged Cross"
2. June Carter Cash—"Will the Circle Be Unbroken"
3. Robert Johnson—"Crossroads Blues"
4. Patsy Cline—"Just A Closer Walk With Thee"
5. Elvis Presley—"Peace in the Valley"

6. The Cox Family—"I am Weary (Let Me Rest)"

Playlist number three included exemplary representations of what I normally listen to, but with the added touch of making sure there was some connection to the project at hand. Here are the first six songs:

1. Social Distortion— "Story of My Life"
2. Against Me!—"We Laugh at Danger and Break All the Rules"
3. The Clash—"Straight to Hell"
4. The Beatles—"Ob-La-Di, Ob-La-Da"
5. Boysetsfire—"Deja Coup"
6. Propagandhi—"I was a Pre-teen McCarthyist"

To be sure, with all of this wonderful music, and you are only privy to a third of it (which is the fraction of angels cast out of heaven—imagine how good the rest of the songs are), I had created the perfect environment for something special to happen.[10]

Most likely getting tanked, but that would only be a secondary effect—not the primary goal. Either way, I titled playlist number three, *Cheers Grandpa!*

It took me a while to finally commit to a number of Saturday mornings in a row, but when I finally did, I experienced something of a rush. The first night I tried it I kept thinking to myself, "I have done some sketchy stuff in my life, but I am so going to hell for this one."

Truth is, I'm probably going to hell for a lot of different "ones," but this one felt unique. You play with fire and you eventually get burned, and here I was stoking the flames. Or, at least trying to stoke the flames. If nothing else, I told myself, perhaps I would learn something about myself, or the nature of good and evil, or the ongoing battle of God versus Satan—something deep and profound.

Over the span of the next several weeks here is what I learned:

1. Owls freak me out. To me, they are the puppet of the bird world. They don't look real. They look like the kind of creature that only pretends to be a bird. Hence, a puppet bird. (Sorry Carly Anne,

10. If you are interested in the remaining thirty-six songs, send a crisp clean one-dollar bill to the "Trying to Escape the Poverty of Student Loans" fund, and I will, in turn, hook you up with the rest of the songs. Send a larger donation and I will come and perform the songs for you—or, at least send you a CD.

I know you love owls, and I think it rocks that you do what you
can to save them, but they still scare me.)

2. A genuine sign of The Fall are mosquitoes, which, by the way,
never seem to sleep.

3. People will drive all the way out to the boonies just to throw their
furniture on the side of the road. I know there is a lot of controversy over the proper definition of what constitutes a redneck,
but that has to factor into the equation.

4. If you cannot drink your Jack straight, at least make sure the
Coke is not flat.

5. Despite not being Catholic, when I have sufficiently freaked myself out (with the help of owls) I tend to cross myself . . . a lot.

6. It looks like I'm going to be stuck with these student loans.

Unlike the ease by which Sam and Dean strike bargains with demons
on *Supernatural*, they were a total no-show for me. Perhaps I was doing
something wrong, but even so I kept thinking they would cut me a break.
After all, I have to be the only Mennonite on the planet trying to secure
a conversation with a demon. One would think they would at least give
props for such originality. Alas, it was not to be.

A disturbing thought entered my head on the last night of my pact-
making attempt: What if they're not showing up because there's nothing
in it for them? What if they assume they already have possession of me,
rendering the idea of a pact redundant? What if my grandmother was
right when she said, "Young'en, sometimes I think the Devil is in you"?

All frightening thoughts to be sure. This remains much of the reason
why I require drugs (the legal kind of course) to sleep at night.

All of the conversations throughout this book, all of the traveling
to different churches, the experiences with fortune-tellers, witches, and
Satanists, as well as my pitiful attempt at making a pact with the Devil,
left me feeling like a failure. Some would probably consider this to be the
exact opposite—that I was incredibly lucky. I'm having a hard time seeing
it this way as many of us are taught that such a being is the primary source
of the world's pain, fear, and suffering. The inability to locate such a source
raises important questions about the way we envision such a world. To be
sure, these conversations, interviews, and experiments were not my only
attempts at locating the Devil, a demon, or even a spirit (those witches
had me excited about forest nymphs). I hesitate to commit this to print

because I know my mother is going to be very disappointed with me, and I could be risking a future tenure track appointment, but I did engage in a few other devilish activities in hopes of finding the one responsible for scratching CDs, creating albinos, and tempting people to watch figure skating.

For instance, and I know this will sound juvenile, but for many people this is the true highway to hell, I played *Dungeons and Dragons*. Actually, it was *Advanced Dungeons and Dragons*. Believe me, I will never make the mistake of leaving off the "*Advanced*" ever again. Talk about a very upset nerd. Sorry, I meant to say, "Talk about a very upset half-elf/half-human chaotic-good ranger."

I also tried a number of spirit or talking boards, or what Milton Bradley calls a Oujia board. Unlike what happened in the film *Paranormal State*, they never caught on fire. When I kept protesting the supposed legitimacy of the boards one of the more skilled practitioners told me I was not asking serious enough questions.

"These spirits are not answering you," he opined, "because they're not concerned with how your student loans are going to be paid!"

"Well," I asked, "if they can't answer that question, what good are they?"

I participated in a few séances. Like the aforementioned experience with role-playing games, I first did this when I was in my late teens. It initially freaked me out. I only did it in hopes that I would get to make out with a girl I was crushing on, which totally didn't happen. I went home, confessed to my parents, and left my light on all night. On a more recent occasion, I sought a veteran group of practitioners and discovered it was not difficult finding a number of people willing to sit down in hopes of communicating with the dead. Unfortunately, they kicked me out when I said, "Harpo, if you're there . . . honk your horn."

Perhaps I wasn't serious enough. Perhaps the Devil doesn't like a jokester. Perhaps the Devil knows I'll be seeing him soon enough so why bother talking to me now. Or, perhaps, as one very devout Devil worshipper informed me, I should have signed a document in blood swearing my loyalty to the Devil along with my renunciation of Christ.

"Is that what you did?" I asked.

"Yes. And then I lit the paper on fire. It seals the contract proving one's loyalty."

"So," I asked him, "what does the Devil look like?"

Appearing confused he asked, "What do you mean?"

"Well, didn't you see him? You just swore an oath of loyalty to the Dark Prince, the least he could do is show up and say 'thank you.'"

He thought about this for a moment. I couldn't tell if he was annoyed by my sarcasm or enthralled by it. He looked around as he fiddled with his sterling silver necklaces hanging from his tattooed neck. He had at least four or five different necklaces that included an inverted pentagram, an ankh, and what may have been an udjat.

Must every religion come so thoroughly accessorized?

He suddenly grinned, looked me in the eyes, and asked, "Have you ever seen Jesus?"

Well played, good sir. Well played.

Epilogue

"Jesus or the devil," the boy said. "No, no, no," the stranger said, "there ain't no such thing as a devil. I can tell you from my own self-experience. I know that for a fact. It ain't Jesus or the devil. It's Jesus or you."

—Flannery O'Connor (*The Violent Bear it Away*)

I could have responded to my last interlocutor with, "I see Jesus often. In the lives of people like Dorothy Day, Clarence Jordan, Desmond Tutu, and Daniel Berrigan." I assume his response would have been something similar, as he could have expounded upon his favorite demonic saints leaving us with competing arguments based on witness. I consider this to be a far more faithful form of truth-telling than what can be found in a theological or philosophical treatise. Biography is indeed the best theology. Of course, for every good Lisieux, Tolstoy, and Francis, there are millions of counter examples to the legitimacy of that which they represent. It is a precarious thing, that which we call faith. I guess that's what makes it so fascinating.

What does all of this mean in regards to my adoption of Tommy's experiment? What does my inability to locate the entity of Satan say, if it says anything, about the existence of God? What if part of the deception inherent within Satan is to lead me on wild goose chases that can only take me further away from the truth that is behind all of this madness? What if Rev. Irving was right and Satan already has me, but has me convinced that he does not have me, leaving me oblivious to the fact that he does have me?

One could protest, however, that such captivity is philosophically impossible because of the almighty reverence we place on free will and the moral necessity to willfully choose our own path.

A path not freely chosen is not much of a path at all.

Or, so we are led to believe.

THE EXISTENCE OF GOD REVISITED:
WHY GINA STILL WORKS AT THE DINER

And to be short, when all the world dissolves / And every creature shall be purified / All places shall be hell that are not heaven.

—Doctor Faustus

The non-existence of the devil is the devil.

—Jean Luc Marion

Historically, many Christians have found it scandalous to suggest that there is no Devil. Such a claim appears to question the authenticity of the Bible, which, in turn, calls into question the seriousness by which one takes Christ. Once you are able to expunge the second most well-known figure in the history of Christianity, it is only a matter of time before the most well-known figure, Jesus of Nazareth, has his status questioned. After all, if Christ did not come to save us from the mess the Devil created, or, from the Devil himself, then perhaps he did not come to save us at all.[1] And if he did come to save us, we must ask, What was Jesus saving us from?

Original sin? The manifestation of the principalities and powers? Death? Ourselves?

Perhaps all of these.

Even if it is a salvation from ourselves, I'm not sure how we could separate who we are from original sin or the principalities and powers. Of course, this still brings me back to the good Reverend Irving. Am I to be looking inward for the diabolical one? If so, the question then becomes,

---

1. Russell, *Prince of Darkness*, 168–70.

How does the denial of Satan's existence alter who we are, or who we think we are, as human beings?

Russell points out that there may be more at stake in the existence of Satan than first imagined. He argues that once you lose the worldview in which both God and the Devil coherently fit, you end up losing more than just that worldview. The eventual result we end up with is one in which the existence of God must, ultimately, be questioned. The process, Russell suggests, only takes a bit longer to get to God.[2]

Though I remain unconvinced that the existence of God is predicated on the existence of God's creation (indeed, classical Christian orthodoxy stridently claims that God has no need for us), Russell may be correct to suggest that, for some, the ability to consider the existence of Satan as mere make-believe can certainly lead to the possibility of eventually denying God. If Satan is too incredible to believe in, what makes the idea of God, a virgin birth, a resurrection, a fully human/fully divine man walking on water and through walls any more credible? Are we therefore condemned to the rigors of a formal consistency in our beliefs, or is it even remotely intelligible to decide, for ourselves, what incredible things beyond verifiable proof we will and will not concede? The former may trap us in a sort of fideism by which our claims are unintelligible to all but those who think just like us—therein, leaving open, on both sides, the doors for xenophobia. If it is the latter, we must welcome back into our homes the claims of Feuerbach.

Perhaps there is another way.

Though no one could point me to Satan, show me Satan, or introduce me to the one responsible for the fall of God's creation, I did find, among the saints no less, racism, sexism, homophobia, fear, hatred, pride, bigotry of all sorts, and a strong desire to make the world in one's own image.

Perhaps Dostoyevsky was correct to say that the Devil is created in the image of humans.

Yet, the ongoing suffering created in this world, not by God, but by humans, coupled with the astounding ability to demonize all that is different, tempts me to believe that, though there may not be an ontological personality known as Satan, surely something satanic exists.

Or does it?

2. Ibid.

In his book *Dare We Hope "That All Men Be Saved"?*, Hans Urs von Balthasar presents a case for why my project may have been destined for failure. He questions the extent by which the concept of personhood can be applied to the satanic being:

> For being a person always presupposes a positive relation to some fellow person, a form of sympathy or at least natural inclination and involvement. Precisely this, however, would no longer be predicable of a being that had, in its entirety, made a radical decision against God . . .[3]

The kind of being I have been looking for is a being that cannot be found to exist.

Following Balthasar, such a being could only be found in the sense that he could manifest himself, in some manner, as a person—regardless if such a person had talons, wings, and a three-pronged tail. But this is precisely what Satan can never do because personhood is only capable of being defined within a grammar that recognizes the other as a person. The very concept of "person" requires some sort of relation that is recognizable in each creature of God as one of God's creatures. Balthasar suggests that within such a linguistic framework, Satan could only ever be an "unperson," because with the radical decision against God (Augustine might call it an impossible decision, therein perfectly clarifying and confusing the matter even more) comes the disintegration of personhood. Balthasar points out that for this reason it is characteristic of the Devil to appear faceless, as his greatest strength lies in the ability to *not* be recognized.[4]

This idea of Satan as an anti-person or an un-person, whose power lies in his concealment, is theologically intriguing. Some would suggest that this is just a sophistic way of saying, "The first trick of the Devil is to convince you that he doesn't exist." But that would, I think, miss the point. Marion's claim above, that the non-existence of the Devil is the Devil, highlights the impossibility of evil within a good creation. Nothing, no-*thing*, can cause evil, and because evil is uncaused, there is, as John Milbank argues, "a sense in which it possesses us like an anti-cause proceeding from a Satanic black hole . . ."[5]

3. Balthasar, *Dare We Hope?* 145.

4. Ibid., 145–46. Balthasar's "un-person" is reminiscent of C. S. Lewis's "un-man" that possesses the scientist Weston in the second part of his space trilogy, *Perelandra*.

5. Milbank, *Being Reconciled*, 18.

What we may want to refer to as satanic must remain impersonal otherwise we forego what it means to be a person. This does not mean that people cannot personally do bad things (or participate in the lack of good indicative of acting on our own parasitic vision[s] of the good); it simply means that in acting upon one's own vision of the good, the person has become a part of something that cannot exist. This person participates in the nothingness that is the lack of good, that is, the lack of creation. It is something that is non-tangible. It is not substantive. This is akin to Christianity's fifteen-hundred-year-old tradition of denying the existence of evil (*privatio boni*—see chapter 3).

In this regard, it could be the same way with hell. Hell can neither be eternal (as the only thing that is eternal is God), nor exist—at least not as a place. That which does not participate in God cannot exist. Therefore, hell cannot be a creation of God, it can only be a creation of humanity—a creation that, since it does not participate in the triune economy of God, cannot actually exist. As Milton ironically suggests in *Paradise Lost*, hell is nowhere. Despite the physical imagery Milton employs for the description of hell's location in the center of earth, Satan attempts to create an empire that cannot be physically located. As Russell points out, Milton's understanding of hell is the "perfect metaphor for the absolute nonbeing of evil."[6] Hell is only where one chooses nonexistence over reality. It goes with the one who chooses nothingness. As Satan claims, "Which way I fly is Hell; myself am Hell."

There is either God or nothingness. There can be no sphere, no realm, no place that exists outside of God. Such a place simply cannot be. Such a claim is often as difficult for the modern Christian to hear as for the non-Christian, as many Christians have fully assumed the heretical notion that there exists something called the secular.[7] The secular is not a place, nor an object; it is only a time. It is the time between times, and it is in this time that I attempted to locate something that simply cannot be located. Satan can no more exist than an eternal tangible place separate from God can exist. Such a separation, however, can exist, and because it is limited to time—that is, it is not eternal—it can only exist as a state of being. As Balthasar puts it, it is an act of the imagination. This does not make it any less real, it just locates it within the parameters of time. Hell

6. Russell, *Prince of Darkness*, 194.

7. See Milbank's *Theology and Social Theory* where Milbank argues that the secular had to be invented in order for modern politics to realize and legitimize itself.

is as we will it to be. This is why it is the province of Satan. As a being created good that has turned against the good, it has, somehow, turned against its own self.[8] It is not only the autonomy of the self that makes hell a possibility, rather it is the invention of autonomy that is hell.

THE PROTEST OF BROTHER RAY (OR, WHY I'M PROBABLY STUCK WITH THESE STUDENT LOANS)

I'm just a simple man, trying to make my way in the universe.

—Jango Fett

It is certainly true that while both Scripture and tradition present a picture of Satan as in constant desire for our embodied souls, I fear that any understanding of God and Satan locked in battle over minutiae creates the kind of dualism that is at odds with the Christian canon. It tempts us not only to fall into the realm of superstition, but also into heterodoxy. This is perhaps no more apparent then in the fatalistic—and borderline *non sequitor*—claim, "everything happens for a reason." Despite most people employing this phrase as a way of feeling better about shitty things that occur in life (and many of these same people still want to claim free will, as if you could somehow have both), it imagines a kind of world that is not the world God created. To assume that whenever something good or bad happens it is the work of either God or Satan is to eliminate the range of possibilities that God created in creation (which becomes even more convoluted in its fall). This is not to suggest it is wrong to be grateful for the good, and think ill of the bad; we just may need to be a little more cautious than the approach of, say, pro athletes thinking God is concerned about their ability to catch a football. For if God really is concerned, let's say, about Steve Smith of the Carolina Panthers scoring a touchdown, then I am led to question why God does not seem to be as concerned about the, oh, I don't know, approximately one billion people having to live without adequate access to water. If God really is giving people such

8. Ibid., 146–47.

as Steve Smith, Kurt Warner, Jeff Gordon, Andy Pettitte, and many other professing Christian athletes the hookup, I bet those dehydrated billion are thinking, "Hey, maybe a little less time with rich affluent athletes and a few minutes over here, please?"

Sardonic-yet-truthful comments aside, all of this is to say that things get quite complicated when such an approach is allowed free reign over a world that, by its very mode of existence, is not only subject to the contingencies of time and space, but *is* a contingency of time and space.

Perhaps the following example will prove instructive. In one of my classes I had a student publicly claim that everything she had ever prayed for had come true.

Can you imagine that? Having every one of your prayers answered? Perhaps some of you can. Perhaps some of you will charge me with being faithless for my inability to come anywhere remotely close to boasting such a record. Regardless, it certainly raises a few questions though, right? For instance, what had this student been praying for that would enable her to bat a thousand? If you had such an ability, wouldn't you use it to end violence in the Middle East, Ireland, or South Africa? Why are we still dealing with leukemia, dementia, Alzheimer's, and diabetes? Why is whaling still legal? Why do people purchase animals when they could adopt them? Why do millions upon millions of people starve everyday? Honestly, what had this student been praying for?

So, I asked. I asked what she could have possibly been praying for that if over twenty plus years of prayer the world still seems as bad a place as ever. Assuming she was telling the truth, I even put in my own prayer request, "If you sincerely think this is a record that will be extended for the duration of your lifetime, I want you to pray for the end of hurricanes, tornadoes, earthquakes, disease, famine, war, people making fun of the fact that I like cosmopolitans, and while I'm being completely self-indulgent, my student loans."

Before she could even respond, one of my other students, a very pious soul of some sort, said, "Dr. York, you can't pray for less hurricanes because they are what God uses to punish people."

Well, that certainly brought an eerie silence to the class.

I wonder if that means the Scorpions should be given credit for writing God's theme song. You know, "Rock You Like a Hurricane"?

Klaus Meine, your countertenor vocals are just angelic.

Angel of Death angelic.

Knowing exactly where this conversation was heading, I asked, "Really? Would you like to give an example?"

"Sure. Take Hurricane Katrina. God had a very good reason for hitting New Orleans with Katrina."

"God hates black people?" I facetiously asked.

Most of my class immediately erupted in laughter. I had to have some way of breaking the tension. One of my students even asked if the flood that hit Nashville in 2010 was a sign that God hates country music.

"No," I responded, "you got it all wrong. God doesn't hate country music, God hates contemporary Christian music."

Due to our engaging in such obvious hyperbole, many of the students were able to see how ridiculous such theological claims about natural disasters tend to be. Nevertheless, a few students still argued that Katrina was the result of human disobedience to God. In particular, God was judging the United States for its tolerance of homosexuality and abortion.

"So," I inquired, "God uses hurricanes to render judgment despite the fact that hurricanes, and other natural disasters, with strong emphasis on the word 'natural,' are rather indiscriminating in regards to whom they injure?"

"The rain falls on the just and the unjust alike," the student responded.

"Easy for you to say, you don't live in New Orleans. But that point aside, a far more faithful person than me once said, 'Far be it from you Oh Lord to slay the righteous alongside the wicked. Far be it from you. Shall not the Judge of all earth do what is just?'"

"I know where that comes from," replied my student. "Abraham is attempting to keep God from destroying Sodom and Gomorrah by claiming it would be unjust for God to kill innocents along with the wicked. Yet, God kills everyone anyways—at least after Lot and his family leaves, because they were the only righteous people there."

I commended her thorough knowledge of Scripture. I am always impressed when my students have actually read the canon of their religion.

"So, what does that tell you?" I asked my budding theological apprentice.

"That if there were any righteous people living in New Orleans, I guess they evacuated before getting hit."

I believe this student had prior theological training elsewhere. Perhaps under a Sith Lord.

Darth Robertson or Lord False'well.

Of course, this is the sort of response you get when you feel compelled to have an explanation for everything. It makes life seem more comfortable, more controlled. Yet, as David Bentley Hart argues, the history of suffering and death in which humans are just as much a part of the natural order as hurricanes, would be even more horrific if such things were morally intelligible. Many critics of religion want an answer to why bad things happen, and many apologists are willing to provide an answer. Sometimes it's God punishing us, sometimes it's Satan wreaking havoc. Yet, Hart reminds us that any answer given only makes things worse. By disabusing believers, as he puts it, "of facile certitude in the justness of all things, it forces them back toward the more complicated, 'subversive,' and magnificent theology of the gospel."[9]

The early church writers were convinced that Satan was probably at his best when he was leading people *not* into role-playing games, sexual immorality, or ethics conferences, but into false teaching. Heresy was a significant problem for the early Christians, and it was the spreading of false gospels that the early church was desperate to combat. It was here where, alongside the arena where many Christians were killed, Satan was discovered to be most at work. What I unfortunately discovered through the countless conversations and research for this book is that heresy is as attractive in this century as it was in the second century.

"So, you see Brother Ray, all I am trying to do is be a good theologian. I'm trying to take 1 John 4 seriously when the author tells us to 'test the spirits.' Call it insane, but a good way to test those spirits may be through a search for Satan, or at least what people think of as satanic. Maybe, just maybe, by looking for Satan I may find out something about God, or at least the current state of Christianity."

We stood there in silence for a few moments. It was kind of nice.

Becoming rather introspective, I admitted, "I don't know. I could be wrong." Genuinely seeking his advice I asked, "What do you think?"

9. Hart, *Doors of the Sea*, 44.

Brother Ray, a man I had only known a short time and who was clearly bewildered by my project, shook his head almost approvingly, as if maybe I wasn't as crazy as he first imagined. He then looked at me and said, "You want to know what I think? This is what I think: I think you had better get awfully close with God if you think you can come out of this search unscathed. That's what I think."

I think he was probably right.

BIBLIOGRAPHY

Alighieri, Dante. *The Inferno*. Translated by Henry Wadsworth Longfellow. New York: Barnes and Noble, 2003.

Augustine. *Concering The City of God Against the Pagans*. Translated by Henry Bettenson. London: Penguin, 1984.

Balthasar, Hans Urs von. *Dare We Hope "That All Men Be Saved"? With a Short Discourse on Hell*. Translated by David Kipp and Lothar Krauth. San Franciso: Ignatius, 1988.

Berrigan, Daniel. *The Kings and Their Gods: The Pathology of Power*. Grand Rapids: Eerdmans, 2008.

Bloom, Harold. *The American Religion: The Emergence of a Post-Christian Nation*. New York: Simon & Schuster, 1992.

Bonhoeffer, Dietrich. *Ethics*. Edited by Eberhard Bethge. New York: Collier, 1986.

Carrette, Jeremy, and Richard King. *Selling Spirituality: The Silent Takeover of Religion*. London: Routledge, 2005.

Cavendish, Richard. *The Black Arts*. New York: Perigree, 1983.

Crowley, Aleister. *777 and Other Qabalistic Writings of Aleister Crowley: Including Gematria and Sepher Sephiroth*. York Beach: Red Wheel, 1986.

Feuerbach, Ludwig. *The Essence of Christianity*. Translated by Alexander Loos Amherst: Prometheus, 2004.

Genevieve Morgan, and Tom Morgan. *The Devil: A Visual Guide to the Demonic, Evil, Scurrilous and Bad*. San Francisco: Chronicle, 1996.

Hart, David Bentley. *The Doors of the Sea: Where was God in the Tsunami?* Grand Rapids: Eerdmans, 2005.

Hitchens, Christopher. *God Is not Great: How Religion Poisons Everything*. New York: Twelve, 2007.

Jacobs, Cindy. *Deliver Us from Evil*. Ventura: Regal, 2001.

Kaufman, Walter. *Critique of Religion and Philosophy*. Princeton: Princeton University Press, 1990.

Larson, Bob. *Larson's Book of Spiritual Warfare*. Nashville: Thomas Nelson, 1999.

LaVey, Anton Szandor. *The Satanic Bible*. New York: Avon, 2005.

Lewis, C. S. *Perelandra*. New York: Scribner, 2003.

Milbank, John. *Being Reconciled: Ontology and Pardon*. London: Routledge, 2003.

———. *Theology and Social Theory: Beyond Secular Reason*. Oxford: Blackwell, 1999.

———. *The Word Made Strange: Theology, Language, and Culture*. Oxford: Blackwell, 1999.

Milton, John. *Paradise Lost and Other Poems*. Translated by Edward Le Comte. New York: Penguin, 1981.

O'Connor, Flannery. *Collected Works*. New York: The Library of America, 1988.

Russell, Jeffrey Burton. *The Prince of Darkness: Radical Evil and the Power of Good in History*. Ithaca: Cornell University Press, 1988.

Shakespeare, William. *The Complete Works of William Shakespeare*. Avenel: Gramercy, 1990.

York, Tripp. *The Purple Crown: The Politics of Martyrdom*. Scottdale, PA: Herald, 2007.